The

Art of
Communicating
with your child

Strategies For Inspiring the 'Champion Mindset'
in Every Young Person

David Chiem&Brian Caswell

© 2009 Marshall Cavendish International (Asia) Private Limited
First published 2009, reprinted 2009 (twice)

Published by Marshall Cavendish Editions
An imprint of Marshall Cavendish International
1 New Industrial Road, Singapore 536196

Editor: Crystal Chan
Designer: Lock Hong Liang

Other Marshall Cavendish Offices:
Marshall Cavendish Ltd. 5th Floor 32–38 Saffron Hill, London EC1N 8FH • Marshall Cavendish Corporation. 99 White Plains Road, Tarrytown NY 10591-9001, USA • Marshall Cavendish International (Thailand) Co Ltd. 253 Asoke, 12th Flr, Sukhumvit 21 Road, Klongtoey Nua, Wattana, Bangkok 10110, Thailand • Marshall Cavendish (Malaysia) Sdn Bhd, Times Subang, Lot 46, Subang Hi-Tech Industrial Park, Batu Tiga, 40000 Shah Alam, Selangor Darul Ehsan, Malaysia

Marshall Cavendish is a trademark of Times Publishing Limited

National Library Board Singapore Cataloguing in Publication Data
Chiem, David Phu An.
The art of communicating with your child / David Chiem & Brian Caswell. – Singapore : Marshall Cavendish Editions,¬ c2009.
p. cm.
ISBN-13 : 978-981-427-610-8

1. Cognition in children. 2. Self-actualization (Psychology) in children. 3. Parent and child. 4. Child development. I. Caswell, Brian,¬ 1954- II. Title.

BF723.C5
155.413 -- dc22   OCN262251236

Printed in Singapore by Fabulous Printers Pte Ltd

David Chiem:

To my mum and dad, for empowering me with their unconditional love and the freedom to dream.

To Catherine, my love, my wife, my life. You provide me with love and strength in a world which requires both. You are the anchor of my life and have shaped the man that I am. To our children, Aidan and Jameson, who are the reason for everything we do.

Brian Caswell:

To my father, whose approach to life was an inspiration, and to my mother, who laid the key foundations.

This book is for my wife, Marlene—who provides the balance and makes it all make sense. To my children Michael, Claire, Nicholas and Benjamin, who will carry on the fight, and to my grandchildren Hayden, Hayley, Nicholas, Banjamin and Bryce, who will inherit the world we leave behind—may it be just a little better than the one we inherited.

About MindChamps®

The second book in the Champion Parenting Collection, *The Art of Communicating with Your Child,* has grown from more than a decade of working to develop cutting-edge active learning and personal-development programmes for young people. Having founded MindChamps® in Sydney, Australia, in 1998, both David and Brian have worked throughout the world with thousands of young people, and trained hundreds of parents, trainers and education advisors to 'make a difference' in the lives of their students.

MindChamps® is a world-leading organisation recognised as the 'specialists' in the art of learning how-to-learn.

Success breeds confidence and determination, and superior technique is the secret to success in any endeavour. At MindChamps®, we have always believed, as Professor Snyder puts it, 'that the champion mindset is a transferable commodity'. By studying the practices of successful people in all domains, we can learn the strategies which have led to their success. MindChamps® expertise is in converting those learnings into proven techniques.

MindChamps'® programmes complement the curricula of established educational institutions. Students are introduced to innovative ways of studying, processing and recalling, based on the latest discoveries from areas of psychology, neuroscience and education, enabling them to develop the grounded self-esteem that only comes with the experience of real achievement and control over the educational experience.

Fundamental to all our programmes is the belief in the development of emotional intelligence, a positive psychology and the promotion of problem-solving and lateral-thinking techniques. At MindChamps®, our mission is to challenge and improve educational standards worldwide, because we believe that the beginning of the 21st century is the time to be living—and learning—for the future.

Further information about MindChamps® can be found at www.mindchamps.org.

Acknowledgements

Special thanks must go to Eric Jenson, Professor Allan Snyder FRS, Mrs Carmee Lim and Miki Kanamaru for their invaluable support and advice during the writing of this book; to Kim Nelson for allowing us to make use of his original artworks; to Kim Nguyen, Daniel Lim and Crystal Chan for their hard work in bringing the project to its fruition; and of course, to all the scientists, researchers, educationists, psychologists and creative minds whose work has helped to shape the ideas and strategies within these pages. Generational change is a team-sport and the role of every individual player is vital.

Foreword
By Eric Jensen

You hold in your hands an extraordinary book.

While some books are heavy-handed or too technical, this one is not. While others are too flippant, light or trivial, this one is not. This one manages to set itself firmly in the thin middle ground.

It is informative, yet not preaching nor didactic. It is easy to read, but it never insults; it always respects the reader.

Finally, it is truthful without being arrogant.

The Art of Communicating with Your Child is full of practical, specific examples of what to do and more importantly, how to do it. This may well make it a classic in the field.

The research tells us that a healthy socio-emotional outlook combined with a 'Champion Mindset' will take your son or daughter much further in life than IQ or any other measure. With this gem, you'll get the specific steps and real life situations in which you can help develop more than just a happy child.

In this book, you hold the blueprint for building a Champion for a Lifetime.

Eric Jensen,
Internationally-Respected Educator
Author of *Enriching the Brain*
Co-Founder of Super-Camp

'The voice of parents is the voice of gods,
for to their children they are heaven's lieutenants.' [1]

—William Shakespeare

Prologue

What Enemy..?

4:00 am. James P lies asleep on the third storey. He is a light sleeper, tossing restlessly, his dreams punctuated with fragmented images of work—of the deal which has consumed his waking life for the past three months.

Suddenly, the pre-dawn quiet is shattered by the sound of breaking glass, a long series of irregular metallic thuds; then the endless, rhythmic droning of a car horn.

He starts awake, his heart leaping involuntarily. His first thought is that there has been an accident on the street outside, but then his sluggish brain starts to make sense of what he is hearing. Finally, he recognises the sound.

It is closer at hand; coming from his own driveway. It is the sound of his car alarm.

Stumbling from the bed, he makes his way downstairs and through the foyer to the front door. Fumbling with the deadlock and pulling it open, he moves cautiously towards the source of the noise, only to stop in his tracks when he sees the car.

His prized Mercedes CLS350 sits where he parked it a few hours earlier, under the portico which covers the driveway in front of the door.

But it is not as he left it.

The glass of the windscreen is crazed and smashed. The lights, front and rear, are shattered, and every gleaming, black panel is dented and scratched, like the aftermath of an avalanche.

Taking out the remote, he thumbs the alarm to silence, staring in impotent disbelief.

Who could do this? What competitor, what disgruntled employee—what enemy—could hate him so much? He searches his memory for something—anything—he has done, which could have unleashed such fury.

Nothing.

For James P is renowned as an honest man. Tough, certainly; a hard negotiator—but this?

He struggles to tear himself from the scene of destruction, and moves slowly inside to phone the police.

But, in the end, he never makes the call.

As he enters the kitchen, heading for the wall phone above the bench, he feels the draft and stops. The back door is ajar.

Then a tiny sound captures his attention—a plaintive, sobbing sound, almost too quiet to make out, but there all the same.

Cautiously, he moves around the centre console, with its rows of cupboards on both sides, alert for movement or threat, but he finds none. Then he sees it. A leg, stretched out on the floor—blue jeans and a white basketball shoe.

The sobbing continues.

Slowly, he moves towards the sound, stepping around the end of the bench and looking down. And his breathing stops.

His fifteen-year-old son, Adrian, sits slumped with his back against the door of the cupboard, and clutched in his arms, supporting his weight, is his father's prized number two driver—its wooden head scarred and chipped, its shaft bent beyond repair. There is blood on the knuckles of the boy's hands, as if he has unleashed some of the fury with his bare fists.

Falling to his knees, James P faces his son, but as he reaches out his hand, the boy pulls away—a reflex action. The look in his eyes is something between fear… and hatred. Then he turns his head away.

James stares down at the blood on his son's hands.

"Why..?"

The single word is a plea for understanding. A question which tears at his heart.

After a moment, the boy looks up. Tears have gouged bright channels in the dirt which coats his cheeks.

At first, he does not speak; just stares at his father as if at a stranger. Then he lets the golf-club drop to the tiles, and the final residue of emotion finds release.

"You never listen," the boy says, as if words can explain the agony. "You never hear me…"

What enemy… what competitor…

Again, he reaches out to his son. This time, the child does not pull away.

Taking Adrian's face gently between his hands, he looks deep into those eyes.

The eyes of the stranger he loves—but does not know.

"I'm listening now," he says, leaning forward to draw the boy to him. "I'm listening now."

He doesn't know what else to do...

How well do we listen to our children? How well do we communicate with them?

James P and his son are a fiction—characters created on the page, with all the strengths and the faults that lie within each one of us. But their story is real. It is based on an incident reported last year in a major magazine, in a major city, famous for its business successes and its self-made millionaires.

Of course, the 'who' doesn't matter—and nor does the 'where'.

What is important is that it happened. And that stories like it happen every day—in cities and towns across the globe.

We spend our lives building wealth, security—a life—for our families, for our children, and we trust that they understand why we do it; what they mean to us. But do we tell them? Do we show them? Do we share—every day—in the moments, the experiences, the joys and the fears that fill their existence?

Do we tell them jokes, listen to their day, take the time just to be silly with them? Do we read to our children enough—or let them read to us?

Are our lives a series of missed opportunities, or do we know exactly when to stop and take stock—of all we have; of just what is important?

"I'm listening now," says James P. And he is. And perhaps it is not too late.

But we don't have to wait until the anger and the fear and the helplessness overflow in our children; until the pressures of school, or peers or a thousand other fears and threats, overwhelm their inexperience.

The art of communication is simple and straight-forward. It is an art which has existed since human beings first lived together in families.

The good news is that, today, with the aid of neuroscience and psychology, we can relearn that art in a way which can make a real difference to the most important people in our lives—our children.

Contents

part one

THE MINDSET ENVIRONMENT

How to Create the Environment that Nurtures a
Champion Mindset in Children

*'Adults teach children in three important ways: The first is by example,
the second is by example and the third is by example.'* [2]

ALBERT SCHWEITZER

LOVE

SELF ESTEEM

UNDERSTANDING

COMMUNICATION

CONFLICT RESOLUTION

PROACTIVE QUESTIONING

PRODUCTIVE QUESTIONS

POSITIVE THINKIING

POSITIVE GROWTH

COMPROMISE

MASLOW'S NEEDS

SEEKING SOLUTIONS

'Be yourself. Everyone else is already taken.' [3]
—OSCAR WILDE

The Best That They Can Be

'If a child is to keep his inborn sense of wonder, he needs the companionship of at least one adult who can share it, rediscovering with him the joy, excitement and mystery of the world we live in.' [4]

Rachel Carson

The world is not fair.

Since the beginning of time, the birth of every child has been the birth of a parent's dream. Who will she be? What will he achieve? Will he be happy? How will she change the world?

As parents and teachers, we want what is best for our children.

Health, happiness and success: these are the common elements in what most parents wish for their children—and what most teachers hope, in some way, to help them achieve.

For some children, the path towards achieving that dream will be smooth and straight-forward—health, prosperity, peace, acceptance and an education which prepares them for success.

For others... the challenges that the world can throw up—the barriers to success—can seem insurmountable. Poverty, hunger, disability, war, prejudice and a thousand other elements can conspire to build road-blocks to success that more fortunate children can scarcely imagine.

Championship lies not in achieving a level playing-field, but in developing the mindset that we bring, within us, to the game of life—a mindset that is bred, for most of us, in our earliest experiences; in the models and the examples with which we grow up.

With the role of model—or guide—comes enormous responsibility. Sometimes, in fulfilling that role, the most difficult discipline we can master is to avoid forcing our own dreams onto our children—to realise that each child is unique; that each young person possesses different talents and different ways in which they can express their own brand of championship.

All we can do is to remain open to their uniqueness; to use our experience and our communication skills to bring out, in each young person, the best that they can be—for that is the true meaning of championship.

Jeremy Lim is, by any realistic measure, a champion.

He can't run the hundred-metre sprint, or break world-records in the pool. He will never, as both his parents have, achieve international success in martial arts. His record of achievement is, however, truly inspiring.

At seventeen, he is an outstanding student, and a veteran public-speaker, as much at home before the cameras as he is before a live audience of hundreds. He has been writing a regular newspaper column since he was fourteen and he was Singapore's Young Ambassador for the National Kidney Foundation Children's Medical Fund.

We met Jeremy a few years back when he was a student in one of our programmes, and it was clear to us from the beginning that here was a young man with the mindset of a true champion.

Jeremy's dream, after university, is to become a writer. It is a dream that he pursues with the same tenacity and dedication which he has displayed in every aspect of his life so far. It is not an easy path to choose, but for Jeremy Lim, life has presented few easy options.

You see, Jeremy was born with OI (osteogenesis imperfecta), commonly known as 'brittle bone disease', which means that his bones have never developed properly.

Both his mother Wong Liang Ming (four-time South East Asian Games gold-medallist and Singapore national Taekwondo coach) and his father Lim Teong Chin (the only Singaporean to hold an 8th dan black-belt recognised by the World Taekwondo Federation and the Singapore Taekwondo Federation) are internationally-recognised athletes and coaches. They had already demonstrated their 'champion mindset' in the sporting sphere, but like any other parents, they felt unprepared for the challenge of having a son who required such specialised attention.

A son, who, before he was capable of operating a motorised wheelchair, had to be pushed in a stroller or carried—at an age when most children were running and playing. Or learning martial arts.

It would have been easy—and understandable—for them to focus on Jeremy's 'disability', and to teach him, by giving in, to use it as an excuse for withdrawing from the struggle to succeed.

Championship, however, is a state of mind.

"When he was younger," says Liang Ming, *"even when he sneezed or coughed too hard, he could get slight fractures... Physically, he cannot excel. So we brought him up to be more intellectual. He has done it against the odds."* [5]

Talk to Jeremy, and you find yourself wishing for just a little of his confidence and self-possession.

"I am grateful," he wrote once, *"to the many people who have touched my life—some have taught me to be strong, some have given me strength, while others have tested my resilience and [that too] made me stronger...*

While many people have supported, encouraged and inspired me, and lent me the courage to be special, I have also had my fair share of meeting people who have discriminated against, bullied or spited me because of my condition." [6]

Jeremy talks openly and unself-consciously of the reactions of others—both adults and children—to his appearance. Like the child who pointed at him and asked his father, *"Why is that baby so big?"* [7]

Far from being embarrassed, Jeremy shares that what made him sad was that the father smacked the child's hand and dragged him away.

"I thought," writes Jeremy, *"his father had missed a golden opportunity to teach his son to understand and accept someone who is different. Perhaps he did not know how."* [8]

Jeremy has the rare ability to look at the world for what it can teach him—to learn equally from successes and adversity. He accepts the limitations which nature has placed upon him, and celebrates the gifts he has received 'as compensation'.

And he willingly shares that he owes much of his 'champion mindset' to his 'champion parents'.

What makes Liang Ming and Teong Chin champion parents is an inspirational determination to seek out the strengths of their special child and to teach him to embrace those strengths and breathe them into everything he does.

How have they done it?

By understanding that the key to discovering your child's strengths is to allow him the opportunity to demonstrate them—through trial and error, success and failure.

Jeremy Lim grew up with parents who gave him as many different experiences as possible; who celebrated his victories openly and with pride, and who discussed his difficulties—the failures and the adversities of life—with honesty and empathy, seeking ways to take the learning from even the most disappointing result.

The old saying advises:

If life gives you lemons, make lemonade.

But the champion goes further. As you set about making the lemonade, why not harvest the seeds, grow more and better lemons and see what else you can work out to do with them?

Jeremy Lim has a rare talent for communication. But how did it develop? After all, he received no premature 'hot-housing' in the art of communication. He was not drilled with vocabulary flash-cards at an early age, nor did he have a speech or writing tutor while still in pre-school—to 'give him a head start'.

The truth is testament to the fact that taking time to understand your child's strengths pays dividends.

When Jeremy was in Primary 4 (about ten years old), Liang Ming and Teong Chin, noticing his talent for communication, enrolled him in an Oral Communications (Public Speaking) programme, through which he was able to hone his talents—to be 'the best that he could be'.

This was not some *ad hoc* decision, taken because it seemed like a good idea at the time. Rather, it was an example of their being open to the signals that their son gave out, and resourceful in their response.

Of course, even before that time (in fact, every minute of his growing years), Jeremy was blessed with a model to emulate; an environment in which communication—open, two-way communication—was the norm.

An environment in which a young child was encouraged to think and share his ideas…

Leading the Mind

A traditional English proverb advises, 'As the twig is bent, so grows the tree'. It is an observation that predicted, centuries ago, what modern science is only now beginning to explain.

In this book, we will investigate what we can do, as parents and teachers, to deal with an environment which is overwhelmingly negative in its outlook, and help the seedlings under our care to grow straight and strong.

Our role, as guides, is to 'lead the developing mind'—to build in our children a positive and productive outlook; a 'Champion Mindset'.

The world is the world, and we cannot control it for our children, any more than they can control it for themselves. We can, however, help them to use experience—and even adversity—to their advantage.

Few children face the immense level of disadvantage that Jeremy Lim has faced throughout his entire life, yet he has developed a mindset which enables him to turn 'upsets into set-ups'. [9]

This kind of learning develops most effectively within a nurturing and stimulating environment. What we will demonstrate in the following pages is that 'leading the mind' is about inspiring the imagination.

At its core, it is about developing our inbuilt ability to communicate with our children.

As parents and teachers, we may never be award-winning writers, famous actors or public-speakers, but we can all learn to be effective communicators—especially with the young people who depend so much upon our leadership.

The Art of Communicating with Your Child has grown from more than half a century of combined experience in the diverse areas of theatre, performance, education, literature, scientific research, programme-development and presenting our popular parenting-workshops.

Of course, the fact that we, along with our wives, have raised (or are in the process of raising) six children and five grandchildren between us helps to put all the theory and experience into a realistic perspective.

Communicating with your child may be an art, but it is an art whose principles are quite simple. Once they are learned, they only improve with practice—and the great thing about learning any art is that the more you learn, the more you realise that, deep-down, where the inner-child still lives, you already knew how to do it.

Our role, as parents and teachers, is to remind ourselves of all the things we understood instinctively as children—before society and our education slowly squeezed them out of us—and then to share those understandings with our children in a way that will ensure that they never forget.

1. Aspiring to Championship

The Mindset of a True Champion

'*Citius, Altius, Fortius*' is the motto of the modern Olympic Games. It is Latin for 'Faster, Higher, Stronger'—but Faster, Higher and Stronger than who?

The other athletes? Anyone else in history?

At a superficial level, perhaps, but championship cannot be measured merely by the results set down in some record book. The true champion isn't looking 'out there' for victory, but inside.

True championship is intrinsic—a state of mind. It has little to do with medals, and even less to do with 'beating' an individual opponent.

On a warm afternoon in 1956, John Landy—the reigning 1500 metres world record holder—lined up with other hopefuls in the final of the Australian Athletics Championships, one of the last major events before the Melbourne Olympics. Also in the field was 19-year-old Ron Clarke, an emerging talent who was already the world junior champion.

On the third lap, with Clarke leading the pack, another runner accidentally clipped his heels, and the young man fell heavily to the track. Landy, who was running behind him, hurdled the fallen athlete, but then he did something that has gone down as perhaps the greatest example of sportsmanship—and championship—in the history of athletics.

As Clarke lay on the track, Landy doubled back to see if his rival was hurt. Helping Clarke up, he waited until the young man had begun running again, then rejoined the race.

With two laps to go, Landy was well back from the leaders, but incredibly, he found an extra reserve of strength, and overcame the deficit to win the race—and the championship—*in a time only six seconds outside his own world record*.

Landy was the world record holder for a little over three years, and the record-books show his dominance of his chosen sport, but for many, the measure of his greatness lay not merely in his record-breaking performances, but in that one superlative act of sportsmanship—that single defining moment.

A successful businessman, naturalist, author and public-speaker, Landy proved himself to be a champion in areas other than sport. He served five years as the Governor of the State of Victoria, and has received many awards and honours internationally.

John Landy remained a champion, long after he finished breaking records and winning medals.

As we set about preparing future champions—which is the role and the privilege of every parent and every teacher—it is important to realise that a champion is not necessarily, or even primarily, a 'world-beater'.

Champions often live wonderfully fulfilled lives, virtually unnoticed outside their immediate social or professional circles. But all champions find ways to excel in what is important to them, and they all possess one thing in common—what has been called a 'champion mindset'.

The term 'champion mindset' was coined in 1998, by Professor Allan Snyder FRS, in a lecture to the Australian Olympic Committee, when he said:

> *'...in my opinion, what makes a champion, and I mean a champion in the broadest sense, is a champion mindset... If you have done something great in one field, you are far more able to do it in another. Your champion mindset is the transferable commodity and not the skill itself.'*

With these words, Professor Snyder introduced a new phrase to the English language—and a powerful new concept to the world.

The fact that many champions excel—and sometimes achieve world-wide recognition—in one (or more than one) area of their lives, can be seen more as a particular consequence of their 'Champion Mindset' than as the defining quality of it; for championship, ultimately, is an internal state of being.

In fact, studies by the Centre for the Mind at Sydney University strongly suggest that most famous champions did not set out to be rich, famous or even successful.

Rather, they set out to follow their 'passion', and above all to stamp themselves as unique—as 'not ordinary'. It is the ability to recognise our unique qualities, to own them and to follow dreams and visions which are built upon them, that is the hallmark of championship. 'Worldly success' is merely an external reflection of this inner balance, focus and creativity.

The sports 'identity' whose life disintegrates once the success and adulation ends; the 'star' who descends to alcohol and substance abuse when fashions change and the studios no longer call; the businessman who accumulates uncounted wealth, but rules his empire through fear, rather than respect, and whose home-life substitutes material possessions for emotional support. These are superficially 'successful' people, but they fall far short of any balanced notion of championship.

We can desire something, or we can *aspire to* something. Desiring is passive, aspiring is active—and, therefore, creative.

Champions aspire. They set goals and develop realistic strategies to achieve them. They have the self-confidence to acknowledge and build upon their strengths—the intrinsic strengths which will allow them to achieve—rather than focusing on weaknesses and shortcomings and using them as a subconscious justification for failure.

If we are to train our children to become 21st Century champions, we must understand this, and train ourselves—and them—to first identify and nurture what psychologist Martin Seligman refers to as their *'signal strengths'*. [10]

We must also learn the important lesson that championship is about achieving excellence through making the best use of the resources we have at our disposal—being the best that we can be; pushing ourselves to the pinnacle of our personal potential and, above all, realising that this does not necessarily mean that we have to be the 'best in the world'.

2. Emotional Versus Material Needs

'Self-Actualisation is the intrinsic growth of what is already in the organism, or more accurately, of what the organism is... A musician must make music, the artist must paint, a poet must write, if he is to be ultimately at peace with himself. What a man can be, he must be.' [11]

Abraham Maslow

Maslow's Hierarchy of Needs

'I don't know what else to do,' the father complained bitterly. 'I give him everything he could ever want, and all I ask in return is a little bit of effort—a halfway-decent mark at school, and a positive attitude to his study. But he can't even give me that.'

A common refrain? Perhaps. But often the problem actually lies in our definition of 'everything he could ever want'.

Too often, that piece of new technology, that fashionable item of clothing, the right brand of sports shoe—even the wide-screen, digital, high-definition state-of-the-art LCD screen, Wii and surround-sound theatre system—represents the 'easy fix'; the reward designed to 'buy' compliance with what we want them to do. And too often the strategy fails, because, at the most basic levels, what we *own* is not what satisfies and makes us happy.

During the past fifty years, society has been constantly devaluing childhood—ratcheting up the pressure on young people to 'perform' like adults—in all areas of life. The demands on young people—from the education system, the media and their own parents—have increased to levels which were hardly imagined half a century ago.

Yes, the world—the First World, at least—is more prosperous. We have more disposable income, more access to credit... more 'stuff' than ever before, but does it make us—and more particularly, our children—happier?

The overwhelming answer to this question is NO!

The facts show that during the past half-century, though wealth has increased, nutrition has improved and educational 'benchmarks' have risen significantly worldwide, the incidence of depression has increased ten-fold in every wealthy country in the world.

Worse still, the average age for the on-set of depression in the developed countries of the world has dropped from 29.5 years old in 1960 to 14.5 years old today.

In Japan, one of the world's most successful and materialist countries, statistics show that, since 2002, the suicide rate in elementary and middle school kids has risen by a startling 57.6 per cent.

With five per cent (3.4 million) of young people in the US, the world's 'richest' country, being rated as 'significantly' depressed (according to the American Academy of Child and Adolescent Psychiatry) and the number of suicides in children between the ages of 10 and 14 increasing by 109 per cent in the past 10 years, it is clear that we cannot make our children happy—or successful—simply by throwing money and material possessions their way.

As American social activist and politician, the Reverend Jesse Jackson once said, *'Your children need your presence more than your presents.'* [12]

The basic needs, it turns out, are far more… basic. And this is not a new lesson.

Over sixty years ago, ground-breaking psychologist Abraham Maslow developed a catalogue of the key human needs which has little or nothing to do with the material possessions which we so often attempt to substitute by way of compensation.

In a paper published in 1943, entitled 'A Theory of Human Motivation', Maslow introduced a concept which was to influence much of the later psychological research into learning, behaviour and social development.

In this paper, Maslow suggested that as our more 'basic needs' are met, we move on to satisfy a range of 'higher needs'—and that all these essential human needs exist in a more or less strict hierarchy.

This hierarchy of needs is often shown as an eight-level pyramid.

In Maslow's model, the four lower levels of need are concerned with our physical and emotional well-being—how safe, secure or healthy we feel. The four higher levels are called 'growth needs' and these are concerned with how we achieve our potential—to learn, understand, appreciate and 'become'.

> According to Maslow, the 'higher-order' needs in this hierarchy only come into play once all the needs that are lower down in the pyramid are mainly or entirely satisfied.

For a more detailed discussion of the importance of Maslow's Needs Hierarchy, see Case Study 1.

Maslow was unusual in the mid-20th Century because his subjects were not 'mental patients' but ordinary, average people. He was not studying pathology, but the behaviour patterns common to all human beings.

This approach was dictated by his belief that: 'the study of crippled, stunted, immature, and unhealthy specimens can yield only a cripple psychology and a cripple philosophy.' [13]

If we accept the truth of Maslow's model, (as most psychologists have for the past sixty years) there is clearly much for us to learn about how we inspire our children to succeed.

Life success is not about making children do things. True achievement develops from an internal desire for growth—a desire which is only possible if the physical, social, emotional and psychological supports are in place.

All of which has very little to do with what we can buy them.

This is not to say that we must deprive children of the wonderful toys and experiences that modern technology makes available. It is simply that we need to look—in this area, as in every other area of parenting—for the ideal balance.

A gift, for its own sake, is an expression of love, but we must not make the mistake of turning it into a bribe—of attaching to the gift strings of expectation (the better performance, the A+ grade etc.).

Bribery like this inevitably focuses the child on the reward rather than the process of achieving the outcome, and any results achieved are destined to be short-lived and of limited lasting value.

To be truly successful, children must develop the mindset which regards learning for its own sake as a pleasurable and satisfying experience. The life-long learner is a person for whom learning is a drive and a passion, and we cannot develop this mindset if we constantly tie material rewards to results.

In our next book in this series, *The Art of Learning How to Learn*, we will be looking in greater detail at the development of the life-long learner, and the strategies for instilling a desire to 'know' in all our children.

If we ensure that the home is a haven of physical and emotional safety, supporting the development of self-esteem, then we have created an environment in which the 'champion mindset' can grow and bloom, and gifts which express our love—without any strings attached—can be a vital element in building this environment.

3. Communication—Bridging the 'Mind-Gap'

'I believe what really happens in history is this: the old man is always wrong; and the young people are always wrong about what is wrong with him… While the old man may stand by some stupid custom, the young man always attacks it with some theory that turns out to be equally stupid.' [14]

G. K. Chesterton

'Generation Gap' or 'Mind-Gap'?

It is an unfortunate fact of life that children come with neither a remote control nor an instruction manual. We learn our parenting skills, as we learn most of our life-skills, through modelling—mainly on our own parents—and this fact has two important consequences.

The first is that our own parenting methods, in spite of the best of intentions, are very likely to be a little *ad hoc* and at least twenty or thirty years out of date, and the second is that the parenting strategies and life skills which we pass on to our children are also likely to be decades out of date—unless we make a conscious effort to alter them, in response to today's rapid social and environmental changes.

The time has arrived when we, as parents and teachers, must develop new strategies—strategies based on solid research and scientific understanding, rather than 'how it has always been done'.

Recognise this sentiment?

> *'The children today love luxury; they have bad manners, contempt for authority; they show disrespect for their elders and love chatter in place of exercise. Children are now tyrants, not the servants of their households. They no longer rise when elders enter the room. They contradict their parents, chatter before company, gobble up delicacies at the table, cross their legs, and tyrannize their teachers.'* [15]

Who said it? A right-wing politician on a 'law and order', 'back to basics' campaign? A 'shell-shocked' educator? A frustrated grandparent?

Actually, it was Socrates, and he was complaining about Athenian youth two and a half thousand years ago.

How about this?

> *'I see no hope for the future of our people if they are dependent on the frivolous youth of today, for certainly all youth are reckless beyond words... When I was young, we were taught to be discreet and respectful of our elders, but the present youth are exceedingly disrespectful and impatient of restraint.'* [16]

That was Hesiod, almost three thousand years ago.

Or this?

'The world is passing through troubled times. The young people of today think of nothing but themselves. They have no reverence for parents or old age. They are impatient of all restraint. They talk as if they know everything, and what passes for wisdom with us is foolishness to them. As for the girls, they are forward, immodest and unladylike in speech, behaviour and dress.' [17]

Words of wisdom from Peter the Hermit in a sermon delivered in 1274 AD.

When it comes to relations between the generations, then, it seems that there is nothing new under the sun.

But does this mean that there must always be a state of 'armed truce' between the generations? That adult-child conflict is inevitable? Or does our increased awareness of human psychology give us 'the edge' that previous generations lacked?

Perhaps, before we deal with these questions, we should examine the actual idea of a 'generation gap'.

Growing Apart or Growing Together—the Choice is Ours

It seems to us that, while some level of emotional tension and conflicting perspectives seems to be a natural part of the evolving relationship between most parents and their children, the issue is not a 'generation gap', but rather a 'relativity-gap'—what we, for simplicity's sake, have termed a 'mind-gap'.

This particular 'mind-gap' is not, of course, limited to differences between the generations; it can occur in other relationships too—as the soaring divorce rates show. Think of all the marriages and long-term friendships or relationships that break down as a result of the partners developing at different rates or in different directions.

This phenomenon is often known as 'growing apart'.

The gap created between them is not a 'generation-gap'—for they are usually of a similar age—but it is most definitely a 'mind-gap'.

And how many of us know and relate well with someone from a different generation—older or younger? Clearly, there is no gap, if two minds 'meet'.

The reason we refer to the 'mind-gap' as a 'relativity-gap' is because young people's view of the world, and their skills at handling the physical, mental and social environment, develop at a rate far greater than that of their parents.

As with most other observations on human behaviour and social interaction, the real answer lies in the perceptions of the individuals involved—on both sides of the 'generation fence'.

We are all 'gods' to our young children, but as their development accelerates (if ours remains relatively 'static'), their perceptions of us also change. As Mark Twain observed a century and a half ago, *'When I was a boy of fourteen, my father was so ignorant I could hardly stand to have the old man around. But when I got to be twenty-one, I was astonished at how much he had learned in seven years.'* [18]

We would all agree that childhood and adolescence are a period of amazing growth in the child's perception of, and ability to interact with, the surrounding environment. We also know that the environment experienced by each generation is subtly different to that experienced, at the same age, by the generation before.

Sometimes, as has been the case in the last three or four generations, that change is more rapid than it has been at other times in history.

If we wish to grow together instead of growing apart, we must make a conscious decision to understand the changes which are taking place in our child's perception of the world—and keep the lines of communication clear and untangled.

What Produces the 'Mind-Gap'?

What produces the 'mind-gap' is the relative rate of change, (that is: the difference in the rate of change, experienced by the child, as opposed to that experienced by the parent).

Consider the following situation:

> At the age of 30, Belinda gives birth to Faith, and for the first five years, although Faith is learning and advancing at a rapid rate, apart from a short interlude of the 'terrible twos', there has been little friction in their relationship. By the time Faith reaches the age of sixteen or seventeen, however, she and Belinda fight 'at the drop of a hat', disagree on just about everything, and can barely stand to be in the same room as each other.

The typical story? A prime example of the 'generation gap'?

If we look at the following timelines, we discover something very interesting:

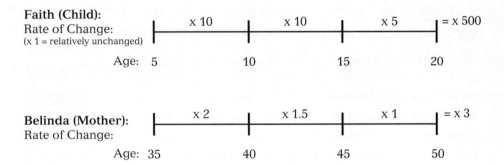

Faith (Child):
Rate of Change:
(x 1 = relatively unchanged)

x 10   x 10   x 5   = x 500

Age: 5   10   15   20

Belinda (Mother):
Rate of Change:

x 2   x 1.5   x 1   = x 3

Age: 35   40   45   50

In the first five years, Faith is totally dependent. Her life is, quite literally, in Belinda's hands. Belinda would sacrifice her own existence, if it meant saving her daughter. This love never diminishes, but it may not remain as obvious—especially if disagreements intervene.

Constant communication is the key. When minds are aligned, communication is a natural process. Of course, if communication is not maintained, the 'mind gap' starts to grow, and once the process begins to gather speed, it becomes harder and harder to stop.

Here is How it Works

From the age of five, until she is in her early twenties, Faith is going through the most rapid period of intellectual, emotional and social development of her entire life. Her view of the world, her ability to deal with the environment, her language skills, her sexual awareness, her social and political opinions, her level of independence—whatever criteria you choose, compared to her mother, Faith's rate of change will be considerably higher. An important thing to consider, in this context, is that the older we get, the more 'fixed' our perceptions of the world tend to become.

The 'mind gap' is the measure of the difference between two perceptions of the same event. If Faith's perception of the world has altered five hundred-fold, while over the same period, her mother has experienced a mere three-fold (or even a ten-fold) change, then the chances of a 'perception gap' occurring are quite high.

High, but not inevitable. With a little conscious reframing, we can learn to build bridges, rather than watching the gap widen.

Bridging the Gap—Making Change a Positive Experience

Many parents have a great relationship with their children—in spite of the rapid rate of change they are experiencing. The secret is the constant effort, from both sides, aimed at maintaining communication and building the understanding which prevents gaps from occurring.

There will be significant differences, of course, but all the studies of the last century and a half have demonstrated that a huge proportion of a child's growth and change is significantly influenced by her experiences within the home environment—experiences which, in fact, bring her perception of the world *closer* in some ways to that of her parents than it might have been when she was five.

What causes the feeling of 'distancing' is each one's perception of the other— their perception of the change in their relationship as a growing 'gap'.

Change is stressful, often triggering limbic (emotional) responses. Couple these with the hormonal, behavioural and even physical changes which the young person (and, to a lesser extent, the parent) is going through, and it is little wonder that the emotions, rather than logic, drive the perceptions of both parties.

The good news is that, almost inevitably, when the child moves beyond the age of thirty—providing an 'unbridgeable' gap has not been permitted to open up in the intervening years—these differences more often than not seem to 'sort themselves out'.

This is a strong indication that what we are dealing with is a 'gap' of the 'mind' variety, rather than a 'generation gap'. After all, if it truly were a 'generation gap', what is the explanation for its sudden disappearance?

We teach our children to question. We ask that they look beyond the old 'truths' and demand evidence—prove the hypothesis; test the theory; never accept things at face value. Why is it, then, that so many parents find it so hard to accept when their children apply the same teachings to family situations?

Wisely, we desire that our children upgrade their mindsets through education. Some families might even move house—or send their children to study overseas—in order to give them access to the 'best' schools and universities. But surely, at the same time, we must upgrade our own mindsets—remain creative, open and flexible; embrace change as change embraces us. When we do, an amazing thing happens—the 'mind-gap' which separates us from our children magically shrinks.

It shrinks because in spite of all the historical evidence, it is not an inevitable state of being between the generations. People of different ages can (and have always been able to) find things in common. Tiger Woods, for example, rated his father as the most important influence on his golf—and his life.

Communication is about sharing—ideas, experiences, opinions. If we are open to sharing, then we can avoid the 'mind'—or any other kind of—gap.

4. How to Avoid Telling a Child or Teenager What NOT to Do!

'I know that you believe you understand what you think I said, but I'm not sure you realise that what you heard is not what I meant.' [19]

Robert McCloskey

When 'No' Means 'Yes'

An interesting and significant aspect of the non-conscious brain is its limited ability to process negative language. Try this experiment:

For the next sixty seconds, I want you to obey this instruction completely.

DO NOT THINK OF THE COLOUR RED.

How did you go? Not so well? What about this one?

DO NOT THINK OF THE NUMBER 007.

Of course, it's impossible to obey such instructions. The moment we attempt to comply, we find ourselves doing precisely what we are trying so desperately to avoid doing.

Does this mean that we are 'wilful and disobedient'? Or 'headstrong and uncontrollable'?

Of course not. It just proves that we are human.

The only way you can consciously not think of the colour red is to think of it, then attempt not to think of it—to cancel it from your awareness. Unfortunately, this is neurologically impossible.

[For a more detailed discussion of this process, read the section on the ARAS (the Ascending Reticular Activating System) in our book *Deeper than the Ocean*—the first book in this collection.]

By focusing on the colour red—which you must do, in order to consider not thinking about it—you have alerted the subconscious search-engine in your brain, 'tagging' it as important. Even though the intention is exactly the opposite, you have in fact created a 'neural feedback' circuit, in which focus on the colour red becomes of paramount importance.

There are four red objects in the study where we often work: the computer mouse, an Indonesian mask and two pictures. By the time we had finished typing these paragraphs, our own subconscious minds, working independently, had each picked out these four objects for special attention.

This is why our choice of language when instructing young people, both children and teenagers, is crucial. Tell a three-year-old, 'Don't touch that stove,' and you had better have some burn cream handy. Before you can draw breath, they will be reaching for the red hot element.

Are they being disobedient?

It depends on your perspective. At a non-conscious level, where the negative language is not processed, the key elements of the instruction are 'touch' and 'stove', so in a real sense, your instruction is being obeyed.

Three-year-olds are not noted for their ability to examine their own behaviours or responses. At this age, their core function is to explore, not to analyse. They don't think about the consequences of their actions, or about the contradiction that exists between the full meaning of the instruction and their action in response.

This is why the children's road safety campaign televised in Australia was very precise in the language that it used:

'Look right, look left, look right again. When the road is clear, cross quickly to the other side.'

Notice they didn't say, 'Don't run into the road without looking'—which is surely the intrinsic message of the ad. And they didn't say, in the manner of some earlier ads, 'Look right, look left, look right again. Then cross quickly to the other side'.

The first version would have seen an increase in child pedestrian fatalities, as children ran straight out into the path of oncoming vehicles. The second would see some children stopping at the kerb, looking in both directions and then stepping off into the path of oncoming vehicles—vehicles whose presence they had in all probability not registered, in spite of their looking straight at them.

Teenagers

But teenagers should be more aware, shouldn't they? They should understand that 'don't' means don't. Of course they should. And they do. Consciously.

But remember, conscious awareness is only a small part of what drives a teenager's behaviour.

The burst of hormonal activity and neural pruning from the onset of puberty through to the early twenties affects more than just physical structure and appearance. Physical change is accompanied by a growth in self-awareness and a quest for self-determination—a need to discover the relationship between 'Me' and the world.

> *For a young child, the world is merely an extension of 'Me'. For an adult, 'I' is an extension of the world around me. For the teenager, the relationship is often still undefined; the boundaries cloudy. 'Identity' is a work in progress.*

In many young people, especially, but not exclusively, young males, a symptom of this quest for identity is a tendency to test the boundaries, and a inclination towards risk-taking—experimentation with drugs, smoking and alcohol, unsafe behaviour in relation to driving, aggression and sex—and in some young people, a potentially fatal sense of invincibility.

What makes this period of development so dangerous is the neurological fact that while the rest of the brain is developing nicely, the development of the pre-frontal lobes (the part of the brain primarily responsible for making connections and forming judgments) is lagging behind quite significantly.

Research suggests that until their pre-frontal lobes have fully developed (in the early to mid-twenties), adolescents and teenagers tend to react to and interpret the world around them with emotional and 'gut feeling' responses.

Functional Magnetic Resonance Imaging (fMRI) scans were taken of the brains of both adult subjects and adolescent subjects while they were engaged in interpreting emotions from photographs of faces. These scans showed that adults and adolescents use a different part of the brain to do the task.

Unlike adults (who demonstrate increased activity in the pre-frontal lobes), the teenagers demonstrated the increased activity in the amygdala and the limbic areas of the brain—the source of our emotional and 'instinctive' responses.

Predictably, the adults showed a far more refined ability than teenagers to correctly interpret the emotions from facial expressions. The teenager was far more likely to interpret sadness or fear as anger—which is perfectly logical, when we understand that the amygdala's primary function is to identify danger and prompt the instant 'fight or flight' response.

Without the balancing influence of the pre-frontal lobes, this 'emotional' response is likely to produce over-reactions during tense situations, escalating relatively minor confrontations, almost without warning.

As we will see later, understanding this basic physiological fact has a significant bearing on our ability to connect with teenagers—especially in pressure situations.

Sometimes tragically, reliance on the same inadequate decision-making mechanism can significantly impair the young person's judgment—even in dangerous situations. This is especially true in situations involving the peer-group. The 'emotional' component of a potential behaviour tends to be amplified by the need to attain—or maintain— 'status' in the presence of a group of friends or rivals.

When considering a jump from a cliff into the sea, a mature adult, with more fully-developed judgement faculties, is likely to weigh up all the factors—the possibility that the water covering the rocks is too shallow; the 'thrill-to-risk ratio'; even the effect a serious accident might have on others (such as family and friends). This consideration will probably result in a decision not to take the plunge.

A teenager, on the other hand, is more likely to focus predominantly on the emotions involved in the action itself, relegating other factors to a secondary tier of importance.

The young person's often erratic behaviour, coupled with more pronounced emotional highs and lows, triggers anger and fear responses in parents, and stifles effective communication at exactly the time when communication channels need to be more open.

This factor adds significantly to the difficulties experienced by the parents of teenagers.

Strategies

So, how do we prevent behaviours which we consider dangerous, antisocial or counterproductive, if we can't simply tell young people what not to do?

The answer has two parts. We must:

a) Use 'Desired Outcome Instructions'

That is:

- Decide upon the desired behaviour in a given situation,

and

- Frame our instructions and questions in terms of the behaviour required, rather than in terms of the behaviour to avoid.

This is a simple, but effective, strategy, and it revolves around our being in control of the language we choose to use.

In specific—often unforeseen—situations, we need a formula for framing our responses. The formula is simple, so write it down and practise it constantly:

Think and say what you want —not what you don't want.

Instructions and questions which promote 'appropriate' behaviours in our children have a distinct 'flavour'.

'*Drive safely*' is a far more productive suggestion, psychologically, than '*Don't speed.*'

'*How do you think you could achieve better marks in Maths / learn to write better essays / enjoy your study more?*' is a far more 'proactive' option than '*Make sure you avoid failing again / making mistakes in your essays / getting so frustrated when studying,*'—even though the intended result of both suggestions might be the same.

b) Guide them to think and respond more rationally, so that they moderate their behaviour more effectively.

To achieve this, we must:

- Prepare and train the slowly-developing evaluation and judgment abilities, by designing tasks and games, and using language in a way which forces the child/teenager to use the all-important pre-frontal lobes, thus 'encoding' and strengthening the neural connections within that portion of the brain.

This is a more long-term strategy. It is achieved by constantly creating opportunities for the child to connect a given behaviour (the cause) with its likely results (the effects), or a desired outcome (the effect) with possible strategies for achieving it (the 'causes').

It is important that the more 'left-field' ideas be given as much importance as the obvious ones, as this promotes a more creative mindset.

Watching the film *Titanic* [20], for example, could provide an ideal opportunity for 'cause and effect' training.

After viewing the movie, ask the questions, 'What were the things that led to the 'unsinkable' ship sinking after all?' and 'What led to so many people dying?'

Which leads, naturally, to the generator question: 'What could have been done to solve these problems, so that the ship didn't sink, or at least to limit the loss of life, when it did?'

This question puts the young person in the position of a ship-wreck investigator, who, like an air-crash investigator, has the job of finding causes, and suggesting remedies to prevent a repeat of the disaster.

It is easy to see how this style of 'cause and effect' thinking could translate to a child's everyday life.

The child might decide that she could improve marks in Maths (the desired 'effect') through revising the formulas, studying past exams, speaking to the teacher after class, forming a 'study group', or any number of other possible 'causes'.

On the other hand, by struggling with the overwhelming notion of 'avoiding failure', the child's responses will be limited and reactive: 'Yes dad, I'm sorry, I'll try' or 'Stop hassling me!'

Furthermore, the focus on the notion of failure emphasises the 'failing' behaviour—placing exactly the wrong concept at 'centre-stage' of the child's thinking, and crowding out strategies for a positive change.

Ethics, morality, judgment, confidence and social responsibility are all aspects of the mature mind's ability to associate—and, importantly, to predict—cause and effect in every situation.

5. The Creative Compromise

'Relativity teaches us the connection between the different descriptions of one and the same reality.'

Albert Einstein

Adjusting the Mind-Frame

Imagine that you have a beautiful picture of your child. Rather than put it into an album, hidden away in some drawer, you decide that you would rather have it on show for the world to see.

Of course, if the world is going to see—and judge—your child by that image, then you will want it displayed in its best light. And, rather than asking one of your workmates or a total stranger to choose the frame for you, you will go to a lot of trouble to choose the best frame. You may seek advice from an expert framer, but ultimately the decision will be yours.

You could choose a round frame, a rectangular frame, even a triangular one.

Each shape will create a different effect, and even the material chosen to make the frame—wood, silver, plastic, gilt, pewter, ceramic etc.—will affect your reaction to what is inside, playing an important role in how you 'feel' about the picture.

Of course, the picture may already be in a frame, and if you wish to change the frame, you will need the correct tools. If, for example, the frame is constructed with the screws on the outside, you will need a screwdriver to undo them in order to reach the picture inside.

Your child's 'mind-frame' on any particular subject—especially one over which there is a degree of conflict—is not so easy to change.

The 'screws' which hold it in place—emotion, opinion, peer-group influence, beliefs, contrary evidence etc.—are internal, and cannot be unscrewed from the outside, no matter which tools you choose to use, nor how much force you are willing to exert.

Apply enough force, of course, and you may well break the frame and get at the picture inside, but such an approach stands a real chance of damaging the very picture you wish to enhance.

Besides, in the real world, only a dictator enforces change without consultation, and the Home Nation should never be a dictatorship.

In this regard, as parents, it is appropriate for us to remember the words of Mark Twain, who, insightful as always, advised us that: 'Habit is habit and not to be flung out of the window by any man, but coaxed downstairs one step at a time.' [21]

Young people respond far better to leadership. Given the right approach, they can be inspired to change.

And how do we inspire change in young people?

We lead them to consider a new 'mind-frame', by asking the right questions—and by allowing them to ask questions of us; to test *our* assumptions. Each effective question from either side loosens the internal screws holding the existing mind-frame rigid.

Once the screws are loose enough, the old frame drops off, and the young person is ready to adopt a new mind-frame.

At this point, it is important for us to recognise that meaningful change in a young person's outlook is rarely the simple adoption of someone else's opinion. Almost inevitably, the dialogue which produces a beneficial change of mind-frame in the child, also shifts our own perception of the nature of the new frame into which the child needs to move.

We might begin with a rectangular frame in mind, while the child appears stuck in a triangular one. Following a dialogue in which questions from both parent and child are answered honestly and openly, the compromise frame might well be the round one.

The Art of Creative Compromise

To resolve conflicts within the family, it is important to develop an environment which encourages open dialogue.

It is essential that all parties feel comfortable to talk, to ask and respond to questions—even to disagree. Most importantly, however, it must be understood from the outset that the primary purpose is to settle the disagreement to everyone's benefit, not merely to 'win' the argument.

Compromise means opening yourself to the possibility that there is a better way that neither party has thought of yet. It is a mindset which must be learned and practised, because it runs contrary to the way we are conditioned to respond in a world where, for countless generations, competition and standing up for yourself have been emphasised as 'survival traits'.

And learning to compromise can be difficult.

It doesn't necessarily mean giving in to the other person's point of view, and it certainly doesn't mean being weak, but it does require each of us to be willing to look at things from another person's perspective—to accept that there is never just one way of seeing things.

It also requires great patience—especially when the other person appears unwilling, or unable, to shift his ground.

In spite of the difficulties, however, it is possible to master the art of compromise—to find the 'round frame' in almost any situation—and to train young people to develop the mindset for compromise; and the skill to apply it to everyday situations outside the home.

At heart, compromise is a creative process, and the quickest way to find the compromise solution is to use what creativity experts call 'the power of cognitive diversity'.

Experts love to use complex words to explain simple ideas!

'Cognitive diversity' simply means that because everyone's mindset is different, they will all see things in a different way, so by pooling ideas, we can multiply the possible solutions and come up with ideas that no one individual could have thought of. It is the origin of observations like: 'two heads are better than one' and 'the whole is more than the sum of the parts'.

Two people applying their intelligence to a problem can create perhaps four times as many possible solutions than either one could achieve working independently. Three people bouncing off ideas can probably produce eight or nine times the number.

If we are focussed on finding a solution to a problem, rather than trying to 'score points' in some imagined competition, a disagreement—or a difference of opinion—can become a very productive and positive situation, and a golden opportunity for growth.

A great leader once said that life presents us with many opportunities—they are like a stream of buses, passing by. The trick is, you have to make the effort to catch them. For some mysterious reason, most people just seem to let them pass.

The champion parent sees conflicts as an opportunity for everyone—parent *and* child—to grow.

Scrabble or Squabble?—How to Create Compromise from Confrontation and Concord from Conflict

If we care enough about a subject to argue or disagree, then it is a good bet that we have some strong emotional connection to our point of view.

But emotions are not logical—more often than not, they are not even conscious. Generally, they simply represent our 'gut-reaction' to a situation, based on our non-conscious response to the world-view formed by our previous experiences. For this reason, our reaction can often be inappropriate for the situation we find ourselves in now.

Unfortunately, the key characteristic of an emotional response is that it 'feels' right. In the absence of any other evidence then, that feeling will dominate, and I will 'stick to my guns' in the face of arguments which don't feel right. And someone opposing me—especially if they too are responding with their emotions—is extremely unlikely to change my mind.

If any progress is to be made, a circuit-breaker is needed.

We need to shift both parties from emotional to logical mode—to analyse, if possible, the reasons why they feel so strongly about the issue.

In most cases, the tool which enables us to do this is Mankind's greatest single invention—the question.

Great questions inspire new-found perspectives, and in order to come up with an answer or support a position, we are forced to use a different part of our brain—to think, instead of merely feeling. The switch diffuses the emotion, leaving us open to new ideas.

Questions control the direction of a conversation, and, carefully chosen, they can navigate us around the emotional impasse, and lead us to the heart of the issue.

Teaching young people to ask—and respond to—questions is, therefore, a key step in creating the mindset for compromise, but a word of warning.

The question is a double-edged sword. Used with the right intention, it can cut through misunderstanding to open the way for the creation of a compromise solution. Too often, however, it is used as a weapon—to 'score points'; to force an 'opponent' into a position of weakness, or a particular way of thinking.

Watch an unscrupulous salesman at work. He will keep asking yes or no questions which lead in the direction he wants the conversation to go, reducing the ability of his customer to resist his 'logic'.

After a given number of 'yes' answers, the trap is sprung, and the sale is made. Whether the customer needed the product or not is often irrelevant, and the customer is left feeling, not elated at the purchase, but cheated or angry—or even defeated.

As parents and teachers, we can easily manipulate young people, by using this method of questioning—and numerous other techniques we learned in high school debating.

But this is not open dialogue. Rather, it is an abuse of power, which the young person will find it difficult to forgive in the long run.

As an adult, my experience gives me the advantage, so I am likely to win the argument—perhaps even 'sell' my point of view in the short term. Unfortunately, it is a hollow victory, which only sets up larger and more difficult conflicts later.

Apart from negative emotions and the sense of betrayal that the manipulation has created in the young person, I have also, through my effective modelling of a behaviour, taught that young person a new way of resisting me in any future disagreements—and effectively created a new road-block to communication.

Effective communication is about opening up the road to a new solution, and used with the right intentions, the question achieves this like nothing else.

The key is the intention with which the question is asked.

If we are going to train young people in the development of a compromise mindset, we must first train ourselves to ask questions whose goal is to build understanding. Only then can we teach our children to do the same.

In order to discover a compromise solution which improves the situation for all concerned, we must first consider all the elements—not only the elements which seem important to us as individuals. To achieve this, we must lay them all out on the table, for everyone to see.

Imagine playing a game of Scrabble.

If my sole objective is to beat the other players, then I will make certain that no one sees my tiles, and I will use strategies that enable me to maximise my scores, while blocking off scoring opportunities and bonus squares from my opponents. In the process, I may well win the game. I can certainly demonstrate my cleverness—even my superiority—with words.

But family life is not a Scrabble game and school—although in many places it has evolved into an artificial and hyper-competitive environment—should be about much more than just outperforming the other students.

This is especially true if we are to prepare young people for a world which is moving away from the 'corporate competitive' model to one in which employees are expected to work cooperatively in teams to solve problems and create new ideas.

What if the object of the Scrabble game were to change? What if, instead of beating the other players, the object of the game was to cooperate as a team to achieve the highest combined score possible, given the letter tiles that each player drew?

How differently would we play?

Each player would lay his letters out in full view, and all the possible moves would be discussed, before a word was placed on the board. Each move would be made, not only to maximise the score for that turn, but to set up scores for the next—or subsequent players.

Compare the outcomes. In the first (the competitive) version of the game, we have one winner and a number of losers, who leave the game i) discouraged, or ii) determined to beat the other players next time.

In this version, the cumulative score (even if one player were to excel) would be significantly lower than that achieved in the cooperative version—in which everyone is a winner, and the team finishes the game with a sense of achievement and the goal of beating their personal best next time.

The added bonus of the cooperative version is that each player, having contributed to the result, feels satisfaction, and the in-depth discussion has enabled even the weaker players to develop their skills by understanding how the stronger players think and strategise.

The same logic can be applied to differences of opinion.

We can approach any dispute as a competition—something like the traditional school debate, in which the object is to manipulate arguments, ask questions and select evidence with the sole aim of winning. This approach will produce a winner and a loser—or maybe two losers—but rarely, if ever, does it produce two winners.

On the other hand, we can learn the lesson of the Scrabble game and 'play' cooperatively.

This means pursuing the goal of achieving the best possible result for all participants. It also means laying all our tiles out on the table, sharing—and respecting—opinions and possible solutions, and asking productive questions designed to open up discussion—not direct it.

The earlier we train young people to ask the right kind of questions, the more effective they will become at solving problems—including those which involve disagreements with others—but it is never too late to begin.

With younger children, the question and answer habit can be introduced in a fun way using games like 'Twenty Questions'—a game which can be adapted for any age group from a six-year-old to adult.

For those readers unfamiliar with this simple and engaging game, the rules (and some of the finer points of play) can be found at:

http://barelybad.com/20_questions.htm#introduction

6. How to Resolve Conflict Situations

'Children have never been very good at listening to their elders, but they have never failed to imitate them.' [22]

James A. Baldwin

Wisdom—A Matter of Perspective

Resolving conflicts requires more than intelligence—it requires wisdom.

Wisdom. The word conjures up images of bearded old philosophers—with the emphasis on the 'old'. The wisdom of Solomon, the Three Wise Men, Socrates, the Supreme Court Judge and the Dalai Lama. Our images may differ, but the one constant remains their age. Ask for a moment, however, why it is that wisdom is always associated with age—why years appear to be the key common element.

The answer is that older people have more experience—more examples against which to compare any current situation—so it is reasonable to expect that their judgement should be more 'balanced'; that they should be able to bring more varied perspectives to bear.

Unfortunately—as we have all witnessed from time to time—age is no guarantee of wisdom. Experience is certainly a component of being wise, but wisdom in any meaningful sense requires something more. It requires a mindset that is open to all the different possible perspectives which may be brought to bear on any situation.

In this section, we would like to propose a new definition of the word, which makes far more sense in the 21st Century context.

If we define wisdom as: **the ability to apply learnings from one set of experiences to the elements of another**, we come closer to the wisdom of the ancients.

Significantly, we also open up the possibility that we can teach our children the fundamentals of wisdom—the mindset which encourages them to search out and balance the different perspectives in any situation.

Too often—as we have already seen—a young person's choices are made with the emotions. Add to this the fact that often, because of their lack of experience, they are making decisions based on a lack of knowledge, and it is easy to see why mistakes are made.

Of course, this tendency is not limited to the young.

Conflicts can be seen as a clash of perspectives—two individuals, or groups, or nations, who see the same set of 'facts' through lenses which are different enough to create an impasse. Neither party can see—or accept—the other's perspective, and the conflict is the result.

Let us look for a moment at the idea of perspective.

Imagine an accident scene.

At an intersection, two cars have collided, in spite of the fact that there is a set of traffic lights operating at the time.

If the streets are deserted, with no one there to witness the accident, then the only perspectives on the accident might be the drivers in the two cars. Each driver claims to be in the right—to have had the green light. Assuming the lights are not malfunctioning, either one of the drivers could be lying—or mistaken—but which one is almost impossible for an investigating officer to work out.

Now, place other witnesses in the vicinity at the moment of impact, and we come closer to the truth. Imagine that there were five people within range of the accident, and by sheer coincidence, each one was holding a video camera. One was standing on the roof of a nearby building, looking down, another was standing next to the intersection, waiting for the lights to change, while the others were standing at various distances down the different streets, which meet at the intersection.

By viewing all the videos, the investigator could build up, from each of the different perspectives, a true picture of what happened—which car had the green light at the moment of impact, and any other contributing factor, such as speed, lights, the use of indicators etc.

Of course, in most situations, the officer would be unlikely to have a video record from even one angle, so he must rely on witness recollections—and as any law officer will tell you, this is not as easy as it may seem.

If the driver's statements are unreliable, because of their bias, each witness is subject to a bias of his/her own.

What we see—or rather, what we remember seeing, which is rarely the same thing—is influenced by many factors, including many which have little to do with the 'facts' of the matter.

If one witness has strong opinions about the driving habits of young people, or women, or old people, it might influence the way he perceives the incident— especially if one of the drivers fits into that particular category. He will not consciously alter his testimony, but he may well remember things in a way which reinforces his strongly-held beliefs.

The witness standing at the intersection may have experienced the crash through the filter of fear and shock—both of which can play tricks on the perceptions—but the fact that she was waiting for the lights to change provides a strong piece of evidence.

The witness on the roof might provide good information about the relative speeds of the cars, but not about the lights, which were not in his line of sight, and other witnesses may have similar strengths and weaknesses.

It does not make any one of them dishonest or incompetent—just human—and an investigator must assemble all the information—all the different perspectives—to come up with a coherent picture of what actually happened.

One thing is certain, however. The more witnesses, the more different perspectives he can add to the mix, the more accurate the outcome.

Wisdom seeks out as many perspectives as possible on any issue, before making a decision or judgment.

Of course, when we find ourselves in a conflict situation, it is often difficult to see any perspective but our own. This is why the cultivation of a wiser, more objective mindset is essential—and it is up to us, as adults, to make the first move towards establishing that mindset.

Albert Schweitzer, the great humanitarian and philosopher once advised: *"Do something wonderful, someone may imitate it."* More often than not, that 'someone' is the child to whom we are such an important model.

Providing the model of wisdom teaches the habits of a wise person, and though they may, as yet, lack the experience or the emotional control to be truly wise, practising the habits of wisdom is an excellent start, which experience and maturing perspective can build upon.

A Mindset for Compromise

In establishing a mindset which promotes the resolution of conflict, we are seeking to master four essential steps.

Step One is for both parties to recognise that what is occurring is a difference of opinion, a clash of perspectives—not necessarily:

(a) a deliberate demonstration of disrespect (on the part of the child),

or

(b) an 'abuse of power' (on the part of the parent).

The idea that we deserve respect simply because of a position of relative power (i.e.: 'the parent', 'the teacher'), may be a comforting one, but ultimately it is counter-productive.

As the old joke goes: *'Children are so unpredictable. You never know which inconsistency they are going to catch you out in next.'* [23]

If we accept that very often we are inconsistent, that our reasons for taking a stand are influenced by factors and prejudices of which we are not fully aware, then we must also accept that from another person's perspective, our stand may be seen as unjustified—even if we are not initially willing to see it that way.

This does not mean that we are wrong, or that they are wrong. It simply means that there is a 'perspective gap' that needs to be bridged, if any resulting decision is to be satisfactory for both parties.

If we are to develop a healthy relationship with a young person, the ability to compromise should not be seen as a weakness; as an inability to command respect. Rather, it should be seen as a measure of strength—both of the individuals and the relationship—that such a compromise is possible.

Young people, especially teenagers, have a highly-developed sense of justice—particularly when it comes to issues affecting themselves. This is due, at least in part, to the fact that a significant amount of their mental energy (far more than the average adult's!) is expended on weighing up their position in relation to their peers and the surrounding society.

Because of their position of relative power, parents can usually enforce their will in any given situation, but compliance on the part of the young person will be grudging and comes often at a significant cost.

Resentment is a cumulative emotion in the young. 'Winning' a series of small battles can sometimes create a war that no one wins.

It is far better to regard respect as a 'mutual obligation', which means that a disagreement is seen, neither as an act of rebellion nor as the exercise of an authoritarian dictatorship, but as an opportunity to better understand the other person's point of view.

Step Two is to establish the real point of disagreement.
It is amazing how often, when conflicts occur, the two parties end up arguing about different things. In any process of conflict-resolution, it is necessary first to agree on what the issue is.

The way we achieve this is to ask a series of 'establishment questions'—e.g. *'What do you feel is the real issue here?'*

This is a two-way process. As the older, more experienced party, it is appropriate that the process is started by the parent (or teacher), but the rule is established from the beginning that any question posed by the adult can then also be returned by—or balanced by a question from—the child.

It is also important to establish the rule that all answers stand. That is, neither party can argue the merits of any answer given by the other person. All they can do, when it is their turn, is ask another question, to clarify. This rule keeps the discussion open and minimises judgement and criticism.

So, the parent might ask, 'What do you feel is the real issue here?' To which the child might answer, 'I want to go to the dance on my own and you won't let me.'

So far so good, the young person's answer focuses on the specific incident in question. But often, this is not the real source of the conflict. In the vast majority of disagreements, the specific incident is merely a symptom of some more fundamental difference of perspective. And it is this difference that we need to unearth, if any progress is to be made.

Now, it is the young person's turn. 'And what do you feel is the real issue here?' To which the parent might reply, 'You aren't old enough to go to the dance on your own.'

Suddenly, the ground shifts slightly. In the parent's eyes, the age factor is significant. Note that the child cannot argue, 'Yes, I am! Fourteen is perfectly old enough to go out alone,' it is not permitted—but a single supplementary question is permissible: 'What makes you think that fourteen isn't old enough?'

'It's too dangerous. You don't have the experience.'

So, the deeper issue is one of safety.

Two questions (no more) from the child, now it is the parent's turn again.

'What is the real reason you don't want me to drive you?'

'My friends laugh at me. They think I'm a baby having my mother drop me off.'

Not just age, then, but 'social standing'—a key issue from the young person's perspective.

At this point, it is tempting to argue with the concept, or to deliver a lecture on resisting peer pressure and being your own person, but this is not allowed under the rules. Only a supplementary question: 'Do you think I treat you like a baby?'

In spite of how it may appear, this question is not emotional blackmail—not as long as the intention is to discover the underlying emotion. If Step Two is to have any value, the questions must be designed to get to the truth, not to play 'mind-games'.

In this case, asking the child what *she* thinks has two purposes. One, it is a mark of respect—an acceptance that she is mature enough to make a judgment on her parent's parenting skills. Two, it is a subtle way of shifting the child's focus from what 'her friends' think to what she herself thinks, so that her decisions and judgments can be based upon criteria that are more relevant than mere peer pressure.

It is a courageous step on the parent's part, to open up her own behaviour for closer examination.

But remember, your behaviour is already being judged—all this process achieves is to place that judgment on a more rational footing.

'Not like a baby... Not exactly. But not like a teenager, either. When will I be experienced enough to have a say in what I do? How old is old enough?'

How to explain a feeling? How to get to the heart of a fear that has no black and white answer? For legislators, it is easy: one birthday signals driving age, another, the age of consent, another the age to drink or smoke or gamble or vote—or be conscripted.

But legislators are dealing with statistical averages—'expert' opinion on developmental stages in a general population. They don't know your child or mine—or anyone else's—at the level of parental responsibility.

Perhaps, the answer to this inevitable teenage question is to step away from the fear and accept it for what it is—an emotion. And just as we are trying to encourage our children to react with consideration—with the head as well as the heart—this establishment phase, if approached in the right spirit, must encourage us to do the same.

There is no shame in admitting: *'I don't know. It's not something I can explain, but when I do work it out, you'll be the first one I tell.'* Which leads naturally to: *'Or maybe we can work it out together.'*

An empowering statement, leading to a shift in the mode of question.

'So, how do we solve this?'

This is the 'proactive' question. It is an invitation for compromise and signals the end of the phase of 'establishment questions' and the beginning of moving forward towards a solution.

Note that the 'establishment phase' has no specific duration—it lasts as long as it needs to last to establish the real issues at stake in the discussion.

When both parties are ready, the proactive question grows naturally out of discussion, and it focuses on resolution. One of the major complaints people is that adults do not listen, while adults invariably say the same about young people. In this case, notice how the questions have advanced the understanding of both parties, without producing negative emotion or antagonism.

It is in the nature of the question to elicit an answer. Questions force both parties to listen. The rules permit no argument or judgment of those answers; therefore there is no room for emotion or pride to get in the way of communication.

Step Three uses a brainstorming process to seek out a workable compromise solution.
This is a cooperative activity, with all suggestions, from the most obvious to the most outrageous, being given equal weight.

Beginning with two conflicting positions, each party now has some understanding of what is really motivating the other. The art of compromise involves considering 'all the options', with a view to selecting one (or a combination) that satisfies the emotional needs of both sides.

This is where the brainstorming approach is so effective.

At the top of a piece of paper, parent and child write the heading, 'The Real Issues (Possible Solutions)'. At the centre of the page, two circles are then drawn. In one is written, say, *Mum: 'How can we make sure Marlena is safe?'* In the other, say, *Marlena: 'How can we avoid embarrassing me?'*

This is a 'solutions' brainstorm, so the idea is to prime the non-conscious of both parties to seek out as many solutions as possible. Together, parent and child deal first with the one issue, then with the other. There are no limitations, whatever is suggested is written down, so that it might look something like the diagram on the opposite page.

Each option is considered, and either discarded or kept as a 'possible'. Some are clearly frivolous (though even a frivolous suggestion can spark a winning solution), some suggestions answer only one issue, some are logistically impossible, but one or two (or a combination) might work as a compromise solution:

- Mum could drop Marlena some distance down the street, and watch her to ensure her safety, satisfying both needs.
- Marlena and her friends could meet at one house, and either go together, or be dropped off together.
- Marlena could even go by taxi or limousine, if cost was not an issue.

'THE REAL ISSUES (POSSIBLE SOLUTIONS)

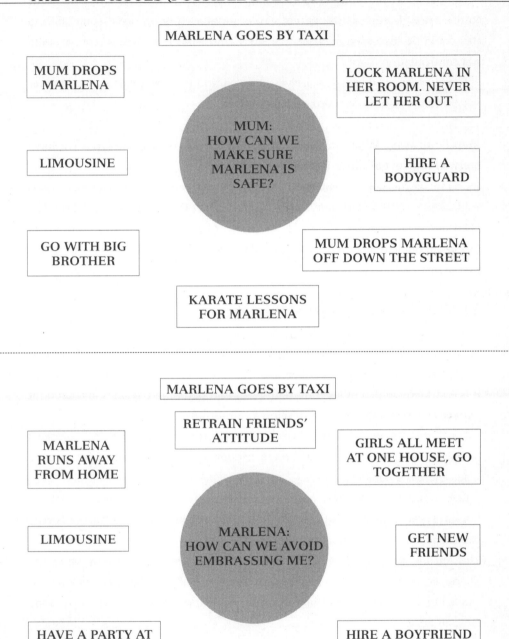

MARLENA GOES BY TAXI

MUM DROPS MARLENA

LOCK MARLENA IN HER ROOM. NEVER LET HER OUT

MUM: HOW CAN WE MAKE SURE MARLENA IS SAFE?

LIMOUSINE

HIRE A BODYGUARD

GO WITH BIG BROTHER

MUM DROPS MARLENA OFF DOWN THE STREET

KARATE LESSONS FOR MARLENA

MARLENA GOES BY TAXI

RETRAIN FRIENDS' ATTITUDE

MARLENA RUNS AWAY FROM HOME

GIRLS ALL MEET AT ONE HOUSE, GO TOGETHER

MARLENA: HOW CAN WE AVOID EMBRASSING ME?

LIMOUSINE

GET NEW FRIENDS

HAVE A PARTY AT HOME INSTEAD

HIRE A BOYFRIEND

MARLENA BECOMES A NUN

Of course, in the long-term, changing Marlena's (and her friends') attitude to the safety issue and the parent's role might well be the best solution, and this could be discussed as a serious alternative—but in a state of cooperation, not confrontation.

The subsequent discussion arrives at a solution that both parties are happier with, and the issue is resolved without anger.

Step Four asks, 'What have we learned and how can we use what we have learned to prevent other issues from emerging?'
Using the key issues as a starting point, the parent might ask, 'What other things embarrass you in front of your friends?' opening up other areas for resolution. The child might reciprocate, asking, 'What other things do you think I'm too young for?' Communication is about understanding the other person's perspective. This four-stage process is one way of achieving that—even in a tense situation.

7. The 'Three-Chair Strategy'

Another interesting way of opening the channels of communication, and tuning the non-conscious to other perspectives, is known as the 'Three-Chair Strategy'. It is a strategy which helps train both child and parent in the skills and thought patterns which enable them to develop a 'compromise mindset'.

The Three-Chair Strategy is a role-play approach which uses the physical location of the chairs as an anchor to trigger a particular shift in perspective when there is a conflict.

Remember that, unlike the conscious mind (which is limited by the amount it can hold and process at any one time), the non-conscious mind contains traces of every experience, every conversation and every emotion we have ever encountered. This means that we 'know' far more than we are conscious of knowing. Therefore, if we can train ourselves to access some of this stored knowledge, we can bring ourselves to active understanding and apply that understanding to the new situation.

The reason we have difficulty accessing knowledge which may help us in a given situation, is because we tend to be limited by our mindset. The Three-Chair Strategy forces us to shift perspectives, allowing us to access other understandings or solutions.

The process is simple. Three chairs are placed in a triangular formation, with two (A and B) facing each other, and the other (C) facing at ninety degrees to their axis. The position of the chairs is important, as it represents, in a physical sense, the relative positions of the various view-points. A and B are the parties in conflict, while C is the 'impartial observer'.

The essential rule of the strategy is that whichever seat we sit in, we must assume that person's point-of-view totally. So, if we were to apply this approach to the Marlena/Mum scenario we looked at earlier, we might assign Seat A as the 'Marlena Seat' and Seat B as the 'Mum Seat'. The 'Impartial Observer Seat' is always the same.

We allow Marlena—as the younger party—to go first, as this removes the sense that there is any dictation from Mum.

As in the earlier strategy, there is no discussion of anything said while the individuals are 'in character'. The purpose is to arrive at a better understanding of each other's perspective, and, perhaps surprisingly, this is better achieved without any direct discussion in the initial stages.

First, Marlena sits in Seat A, facing 'Mum' (the empty Seat B). From this position, she is free to tell her mother anything she feels about the situation in question.

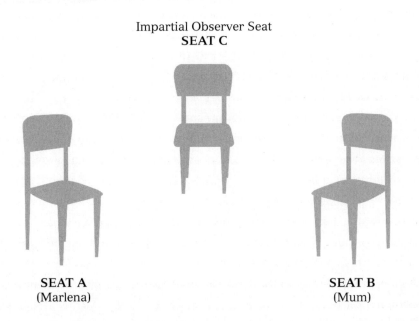

Impartial Observer Seat
SEAT C

SEAT A
(Marlena)

SEAT B
(Mum)

She is establishing her perspective, giving voice to the emotions she is feeling, explaining things she would like her mother to understand—but which she might not be able to voice were she actually talking directly to her mother.

'You treat me like a child,' she might say. 'I'm fourteen and you don't allow me any freedom. Do you know how embarrassing it is to have your mother drop you off in front of all your friends? You never look at things from my point of view. How can I learn responsibility, if you don't allow me any? Elizabeth gets to travel all the way into the city on her own, and she never gets into any trouble. Her parents trust her. I can't even go to a school dance without my 'chaperone' dropping me off and picking me up. It's ruining my reputation. They're all calling me 'baby' and 'Mummy's girl', and it's embarrassing. You have to let me grow up…'

It is difficult to look at issues from another person's perspective, particularly for young people. Marlena now moves to sit in Seat B, 'Mum's seat', and the physical act of moving, of assuming the role of Mum and facing back towards 'herself', is designed to promote a shift in point of view.

Remember, the non-conscious mind works on a symbolic level, which is why the concept of role-playing works so well. Knowledge which Marlena may not be able to access may well be available to 'Marlena-as-Mum'. This is because the act of moving seats 'reprogrammes' the priorities of the non-conscious. It is now primed to seek out those elements of particular importance to 'Marlena-as-Mum'—and these will include comments and whole conversations which Marlena ignored previously, or which failed entirely to register.

People attempting the Three-Chair Strategy for the first time are often amazed at the insight they achieve, without prompting from any outside source.

'Marlena-as-Mum' might well say, 'It's my job to worry about you. You're still a kid. You don't have the experience to handle what might happen. The world is a dangerous place, far more dangerous than it was when I was your age, and just because Elizabeth's parents don't care, doesn't mean that I'm going to ignore the facts. As long as I'm in charge, I will decide when you're 'old enough'. And you'll just have to accept it.'

Now, it is Mum's turn. We could allow Marlena to go straight into the 'impartial observer' role, but it is important for her to be in possession of as much information as possible before judgments are formed.

Much of what she has said as 'Marlena-as-Mum' is merely repetition of what she has heard earlier. It is now at the front of her mind, which is a good start, but before the judgment of the 'impartial observer' becomes cemented as the paradigm upon which future decisions will be made, we want to ensure that it is fully understood—from Mum's perspective, as well as her own.

First, Mum sits in Chair B.

'*I know, you think you're grown-up,*' she might say, '*but I don't want to see you getting hurt, if there is any way I can protect you. I know it's hard to hear what your friends have to say, but will they be there, if anything goes wrong? You should learn to be yourself and not worry about what other people say. Do you think I take a stand just to annoy you; just to prove that I'm the boss? It isn't that easy being the parent. One day you'll understand that.*'

Moving now to Chair A, Mum assumes the role of Marlena.

'*It's not easy being the kid either,*' she might begin. '*There's so much I want to do that I can't. So many places I want to go. I want to be able to prove myself, but you don't want to let me. I know you are scared for me, but you can't live my life for me forever, and if you don't give me some responsibility, how am I ever going to learn to be responsible? There must be some way for you to let me off the leash and still feel safe.*'

At the end of the process, when first Marlena, then Mum, sits in the 'impartial observer' chair, they will each be prepared to entertain a compromise perspective, creating more common ground between them, which should result in some mutually acceptable changes.

Again, this is achieved without direct confrontation, and without either party attacking statements, beliefs or values expressed by the other. The advantage is that each, in the role of impartial observer, reaches a compromise perspective, through her own intellectual effort and this cements that perspective far more effectively than if it had been imposed from outside.

The Three-Chair Strategy is particularly effective when the source of conflict is not specific. Whenever there is tension in a relationship, it is useful for both parties to 'open' their perspectives, so that meaningful dialogue can take place.

A Variation

A useful variation on the Three-Chair Strategy can be used if there is a third impartial party (someone not directly involved in the disagreement). It can also be used if the two in conflict are children, and the parent wishes to achieve a controlled discussion of the issue.

In this variation, the third person sits in the impartial observer's seat, while the other two sit facing each other. The observer controls the session, through the use of proactive questions, and the use of the 'switch option'.

If Adam and Bernice are in conflict, we might call 'Seat A' Adam's seat, and 'Seat B' Bernice's seat. Each begins the session seated in his/her own seat, and the neutral observer begins by asking first one, then the other, 'What do you feel is the issue here?'

As in other strategies, there is no direct discussion of the other person's statements. When both participants have given their point of view, the observer can ask supplementary questions, designed to develop what they have already revealed.

At any time, the observer can say 'Switch!'—which is the signal for the two participants to swap seats, and try to see things from the opposite point of view.

Like the original Three-Chair Strategy, the process encourages two people in conflict to listen to—and understand—the other person's point of view, and sometimes the presence of the neutral observer is a great benefit in opening up lines of discussion. This is especially true if the people in conflict are inexperienced at expressing their ideas aloud.

8. How to Create 'Positive Growth' and a Healthy 'Self-Image' in Young People

'You yourself, as much as anybody in the entire universe, deserve your love and affection.' [24]

Buddha

Filling the Bucket

Our self-image does not exist or develop in a vacuum. It grows as a result of our social interactions from the day we are born until the day we die. This is the truth behind the famous piece of timeless wisdom:

> *'We are not who we think we are. We are not who others think we are. We are who we think others think we are.'*

For children and teenagers, one of the key sources of self-image is the home, and this makes the parent's/teacher's role as 'self-image facilitator' a crucial one.

Another anonymous author once commented, 'Parents need to fill a child's bucket of self-esteem so high that the rest of the world can't poke enough holes in it to drain it dry.'

But this cannot be achieved simply by pouring in a constant stream of unfounded praise. Children know when praise is warranted—and when it isn't—and false or excessive praise is one of the most obvious forms of patronising adult behaviour. Patronising and potentially counter-productive.

At best, it is a meaningless and slightly embarrassing ordeal for the child—especially if encountered in a public or semi-public situation. At worst, if used constantly, it creates an expectation of undeserved reward—which feeds on itself, creating an escalating demand cycle.

In this, as in many things, we can look back over the millennia to the wisdom of Aristotle, who assures us that, 'Dignity does not consist in possessing honours, but in deserving them.' [25]

In *Charlie and the Chocolate Factory* by Roald Dahl, Veruca Salt, the spoiled little rich girl is annoying and demanding—and ultimately pitiable—because her father constantly feels the need to praise her and reward her, simply for being his 'beautiful' daughter. She is a caricature, of course—but caricatures, when they work, succeed because they are based on universal truths.

In Veruca, we recognise our own failings or those of other parents who have made the mistake of relying on unfounded praise and reward strategies to 'build-up' their child's self-esteem.

At a more subtle level, this is exactly the mistake made by many motivational programmes—usually taking the form of a two-, three- or five-day camp, during which the children and adolescents are exposed to a high-pressure stream of self-esteem and study strategies, designed to focus them on their goals and convince them that they are inevitably destined for success.

Telling children they are capable of anything, programming them with 'feel-great' affirmations and convincing them that 'anything is possible if you just believe' is fine—if you also provide them with the tools to achieve the results. But these tools of emotional, social, academic and intellectual growth develop slowly, and take careful inculcation.

The apparent 'improvements' achieved in two-, three- or five-day programmes are based not on any fundamental change in the way the child learns, but rather on the easily-stimulated buzz of a high-powered motivational session. For any permanent growth to occur, the child needs to take ownership of practical tools that enable him/her to continue growing.

Such an approach changes the surface belief—and therefore the outward demeanour—of the child, so it is easy to believe that some 'miraculous' change has taken place. But this is (as psychologist Martin Seligman described it), 'footless self-esteem' [26], doomed to failure by its very nature.

The real test, of course, comes in the weeks and months following. Does the motivation last? Is the 'improvement' permanent—or a temporary peak?

Throwing out a few 'handy hints' in the form of 'super-study strategies' without the resources to allow for adequate reinforcement, application and reiteration over time does not count as adequate preparation.

Once the 'positive mindset' has been established, careful training is needed in the processes required to accomplish the change in social and educational outcomes that is needed to sustain the new 'self-image'. After all, at this stage it is merely a vision of future potential—one that has been artificially induced by the high-powered motivational sessions and the 'group-psychology' of the programme.

Soundly-based programmes do not aim for the quick-fix, but for permanent and demonstrable change—for life.

Self-image is a constantly evolving and fragile entity, and to artificially impose it is not so very different to the parental mistake of providing false-praise or unearned rewards. The child comes back from the camp with enhanced confidence and a belief that success is inevitable, but without a solid grasp of the skills and techniques necessary to achieve the promised results, soon experiences the set-backs, which are an inevitable part of life.

But set-backs are not part of the promise. 'Visualisation of goals' is presented as a magic talisman. If I imagine success, it is supposed to happen.

When it doesn't, something or someone must be to blame. Maybe it's the school, the teachers, my parents. Maybe it's me. Maybe I'm just not the 'successful type'.

Gradually, the confidence dissipates, the self-esteem slips, and the sense of failure grows, until all the enthusiasm is lost, and the child goes back to the old habits, but with an increased sense of inadequacy.

There is a huge difference between motivation and inspiration. Motivation is external—it is something we do to someone—and as such, once the motivating activity ceases, so does the effect.

Like the tempest which changes the very nature of the sea, motivation appears to be powerful and overwhelming. But what happens when the wind dies away? The sea swiftly returns to the way it was, with only some flotsam and jetsam on the seashore to indicate it was ever any other way.

So, too, with motivation. When the hype is over, and real life reasserts itself, all that is left are a few remaining pools of self-belief, slowly evapouring in the sun.

Inspiration is different. Inspiration is about changing the currents and the tides of a person's life; and making permanent changes—from the inside. The verb 'to inspire' comes from the Latin spirare meaning 'to breathe' and has been used since the Middle Ages to refer to the divine infusion into a person of a feeling or an idea—hence: 'divine inspiration'.

Our role—as parents or teachers—is not to provide a temporary disturbance to the surface of our children's lives, but to encourage and *inspire* them to look down deep inside themselves to find the strength and uniqueness that will transform them *permanently* into the champions that they were born to be.

How to Create Sustainable Change

In *Deeper than the Ocean,* we looked at the nature of successful and permanent change, and explained it using this diagram:

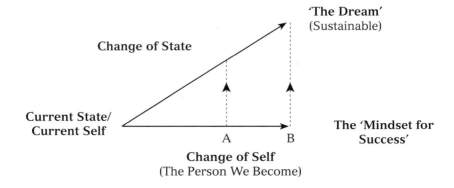

The greater the change in myself, the greater the sustainable change in my 'state' that I can support long-term. Healthy self-esteem is built on a foundation of self-respect, which, in turn, grows from pride in achievement.

Respect—especially self-respect—must be earned. If we achieve a goal, our self-esteem is boosted. If, subsequently, our efforts are appreciated, we feel a pride in our accomplishment.

Helping others, sharing ourselves without the expectation of any reward, is one of the most satisfying ways of building self-respect—which, of course, is the origin of the truism, 'It is better to give than to receive.'

As parents or teachers, we can easily create opportunities for children and young people to do something concrete and meaningful for others—especially if we, too, provide a model through our own behaviour and actions. Establishing the 'caring and sharing' habit in our children from a young age is of immense advantage to their self-esteem as they grow—especially if it is seen as a normal part of life, as opposed to a rare behaviour that is especially commented upon and followed by external reward.

Rather than unfounded praise and rewards, rather than the artificial 'build-up' of a short—and expensive—motivational programme, a better long-term strategy is to create an environment at home that will promote a healthy and sustainable development of the child's self-image. The key to achieving this is, as we touched upon earlier, to keep open the lines of communication.

In Part Two, we will examine some strategies for achieving exactly that result.

HOW TO APPLY THE KNOWLEDGE

Exercise 1. Maslow's Needs: What Can We Learn from Abraham Maslow?

In Case Study 1, we examine the Hierarchy of Human Needs, which Abraham Maslow developed more than half a century ago. By understanding the basic principles behind his discovery, we can understand much of what drives our children's behaviour—and what we can do to help them.

If the physical needs and the needs for safety, emotional security and self-esteem are all being met, then we have created the situation in which the child is able to grow. This is because the growth needs—the need to know and understand; the need for aesthetic appreciation (enjoyment) of the world around us; the need to achieve all that we can and the need to transcend our ordinary selves—only drive our actions once the basic physical, emotional and esteem needs have been met.

As parents and teachers, we can learn to focus on the basic needs of the young people who depend upon us. If we make certain that the 'basic needs' are met, then the 'growth needs' become the 'drivers of behaviour'—especially learning behaviour.

One effective way to do this is to fill in the following table, taking into account all the things which might affect the child's physical, emotional and psychological state. Make a copy of the table for each child—as each child's needs are different.

When deciding on a rating for Column 2, it is easiest to use the key:

1—Always Satisfied

2—Often / Usually Satisfied

3—Sometimes Satisfied

4—Rarely Satisfied

5—Never Satisfied

NEED	RATING	REMEDY
PHYSICAL		
Hunger/Thirst		
Environment		
Sleep*		
General Health		

SAFETY		
Physical		
Relational		
Emotional		
Material		
LOVE/ BELONGING		
Family		
Friends/Peers		
Other groups		
Romantic		
ESTEEM		
Self		
Family		
Social		

If the young person scores a rating of 3–5 in any area, then it indicates that some remedy is necessary. Setting things out in this manner helps us to recognise the need for action, which we can then brainstorm until a remedy suggests itself.

*Take 'Sleep' for example:

When calculating the adequate amount of sleep, it is important to understand that it is not just the number of hours that is important, but when those hours are taken. Due to the body's circadian rhythms (sleep patterns)—which are influenced by automatic internal responses to the external environment (light, temperature etc.)—the body prepares itself for sleep at around sunset, and begins to prepare for waking a little before sunrise.

One result is that it becomes harder and harder to concentrate and think the later it gets at night because the brain chemicals released in preparation for sleep dampen the ability to focus. They dull the brain.

Add this to the fact that the 'deep-sleep zone' is the most important state for cell regeneration and long-term memory formation, and the timing of sleep becomes crucial.

As a rough rule of thumb, it can be estimated that one hour of sleep between sunset and 2 am is worth two hours of sleep after that time. So, if we call any hour after 2 am one unit of sleep, then any hour between sunset and 2 am would represent two units. For school-age children and adolescents, we should be aiming for an absolute minimum of 12 units per night, so let's see how different bedtimes affect the equation:

- Sleeping 9 pm to 6 am (9 hours) equates to 5 hours before 2 am (10 units) plus 4 hours after 2 am (4 units) a very healthy total of 14 units.

- Sleeping 10 pm to 7 am (9 hours) equates to 4 hours before 2 am (8 units) plus 5 hours after 2 am (5 units) a still healthy total of 13 units.

- Sleeping 11 pm to 7 am (8 hours) equates to 3 hours before 2 am (6 units) plus 5 hours after 2 am (5 units) an inadequate total of 11 units.

- Sleeping midnight to 8 am (8 hours) equates to 2 hours before 2 am (4 units) plus 6 hours after 2 am (6 units) a severely inadequate total of only 10 units.

But of course, few children can afford to sleep in that late, so if they go to sleep at midnight or later, they will probably only manage a dangerously low 7 or 8 units.

For a parent to allow this to happen consistently is bordering on negligence. Not only is this amount of sleep inadequate, severely affecting their academic performance, but it is also very unhealthy in the long-run—sleep-deprivation being directly linked to hypertension, cardio-vascular disease, obesity, depression and diabetes in international studies.

If your child (indeed anyone) consistently scores below 12 units per night, then some remedy is urgently needed.

This simple, logical approach to sleep times is of particular importance during periods of study stress—when a child is 'cramming' for an external exam, for example.

Sleeping at 9.30 pm and waking at 6 am (13 units) to continue studying for two hours, when the mind is fresh and receptive, and the brain has had a chance to properly process last night's information, is far better than the illogical, emotional drive to study—inefficiently, in a highly-fatigued state—until midnight then waking at 8 am (10 units) to rush to school, tired and unable to focus effectively on the day ahead.

Using the Maslow's Needs criteria, we can recognise various areas of concern, and better equip ourselves to prepare our children for growth—in all areas of their lives.

Exercise 2. Using The Best Language

We have seen how the non-conscious mind finds it difficult to process negative words such as 'don't'.

Identify three phrases that you use with your child that include the word 'don't', or a similar negative word.

Translate each of these phrases into a 'desired outcome instruction'.

Examples:

"Don't run" becomes "Walk carefully"

"Don't throw your clothes on the floor!" becomes "Please put your clothes in the washing basket."

Daily Habit: Each time you find yourself using the word 'don't' with your child, follow it immediately with a 'desired outcome' instruction phrase that is designed to achieve the same purpose. Gradually, the positive mode of expression will replace the negative one as a verbal process.

Exercise 3. Using Proactive Questions

Consider areas in which you would like your child to improve. Choose three areas and think of three questions that you could pose to your child. Questions should start with, "How is it possible to improve..."

Examples:

- How is it possible to improve your writing?

- How is it possible to improve the way you play with your sister?

- How is it possible to improve your jump-shot?

  Choose one of these questions and ask your child the four proactive questions

1. How is it possible to improve... (your writing)?

2. What are the consequences (What will happen) if you improve... (your writing)?

3. What are the consequences (What will happen) if you don't improve... (your writing)?

4. What are the things that are stopping you from improving... (your writing) and how can we overcome those things?

Take question 4 and turn it into a brainstorm to surface all of the things that are obstacles to your child's improvement. Once you have surfaced all of those things, rank them in the order of how actively each 'obstacle' stops the desired improvement from occurring. Then take the most active obstacle and create a brainstorm seeking strategies to overcome that obstacle.

Daily Habit: Make it a daily habit to ask your child 'how' and 'what' questions as opposed to 'why' questions. Challenge your child to reframe 'why' questions as 'how' and 'what' questions.

Exercise 4. Resolving Conflict

When a conflict arises with your child, find a suitable time to sit down together and have a conversation to understand each other and resolve the conflict. Explain to your child that the purpose of the conversation is for you to understand how they feel and for them to understand how you feel about the issue. Use 'establishment questions' to establish the source and extent of the conflict.

Explain the rules:

1. The first question from each person should be, "What do you feel the real issue is?"

2. Questions should ideally start with 'what' or 'how'. They should not start with 'why'.

3. The answers each person makes cannot be challenged or directly discussed. Neither party can disagree with the other party's answers.

4. Each person asks a maximum of two questions at a time.

   Apply the Three-Chair Strategy. As a starting version you might choose to simply swap chairs after your 'establishment question' conversation and state your understanding of what the other person feels is the issue. The statement should be made in the first person, as if you are the other person (eg: "I feel the real issue is…"). Alternatively, you may have a third person sit in a neutral chair and ask both parties to swap seats and answer the question; "What do you feel is the real issue?"—from the other person's point of view.

   As this process becomes more familiar, you can expand it to encompass the full Three-Chair Strategy.

part two

HOW TO CREATE THE 'COMMUNICATION HABIT'

Adult-Child Communication Strategies

'As adults, we must ask more of our children than they know how to ask of themselves... [We must] show them ways they can connect, reach out, weave themselves into the web of relationships that is called community.' [27]

DAWNA MARKOVA

FOUR GOLDEN
RULES

DESCRIPTIVE
PRAISE

DEVELOPING
AWARENESS

PAYING
ATTENTION

MAINTAINING
CONNECTION

CREATING
RAPPORT

*'Don't worry that your children
never listen to you, worry that
they are always watching you.'* [28]
ROBERT FULGHUM

The Leader of Three Thousand Men

A couple of years ago, a business associate asked David if he would mind speaking to a friend who was having some difficulties with his teenage son.

The man was clearly troubled by the situation, and in the course of the conversation confided, "Every day, I make important decisions which affect the lives of over three thousand men—but I can't talk to my own son. He doesn't even want me to drop him off at school."

"Tell me," David began, "how long have you worked at your company?"

"Almost thirty years," came the reply.

"And how many days a week would you say you work, on average?"

"Five, maybe six. Usually six."

"And how many hours a day?"

"Ten, twelve, thirteen. Sometimes even more. Not like the kids of today. They don't know what hard work is."

"So, you've worked five or six days a week, at least ten hours a day, for thirty years. That's tens of thousands of hours spent learning how to do what you're so good at. And in that time, how many books do you think you've read on management and other related areas?"

"I don't know. Quite a few, I guess."

"So, you've worked five or six days a week, at least ten hours a day, for thirty years, and you've read quite a few books to develop your ability to lead three thousand men. Tell me, how much time have you spent learning how your son's mind works, and how to lead your son?"

For this question, the man had no answer.

If we are being honest, how many of us could answer that question in a satisfactory way? If we are to be their guides, their role models, how much time should we spend preparing ourselves for such an important job?

Is anything in our lives more important than that role?

1. The Four 'Golden Rules' for Inspired and Inspiring Communication with Your Child

'The best brought-up children are those who have seen their parents as they are. Hypocrisy is not the parents' first duty.' [29]

George Bernard Shaw

Karl Gustav Jung—one of the 20th Century's most influential and insightful thinkers in the field of developmental psychology—wrote:

> *'If there is anything that we wish to change in the child, we should first examine it and see whether it is not something that could better be changed in ourselves.'* [30]

Our role as adults is to inspire and guide—especially in times of high pressure—and we can only achieve this if the channels of communication remain open.

This part of the book looks at the Four Golden Rules of Communication with young people:

1. Be Aware of the Young Person's 'Processing Limitations'
2. Give Your Full Attention to All the Possibilities in a Communication Situation—No Matter What the Distractions
3. Balance Praise and Criticism—Provide Support While Encouraging Independence
4. Develop Strategies for Controlling the Negative Emotion in Any Situation

Mastery of these Four Golden Rules can and does open the door to better communication between parents/teachers and the most important people in their lives. How many of them do you follow?

GOLDEN RULE NUMBER ONE: BE AWARE OF THE YOUNG PERSON'S 'PROCESSING LIMITATIONS'

When talking with your child or teenager:

i)   Ask just one question at a time.

ii) Allow the young person to finish speaking, instead of attempting to anticipate his/her answers.

iii) Avoid the temptation to interrupt his/her answers, even if the words suggest a response.

Young people are not built as well as adults to cope with stress, due to the fact that the pre-frontal cortex of their brain is still developing. They are, therefore, far more likely to respond with their 'unthinking' emotions than with their logical faculties when challenges arise.

This means that we—as the adult—must be the ones to control the situation, and avoid creating unnecessary frustration. Inspiration is about empowering the young person to achieve and we can only do this if we are communicating effectively—and without emotional misunderstanding.

Asking 'Double-Barrelled' Questions:

If we ask two or more part-questions, we will probably only get the answer to one part—and very likely set up a defensive reaction, which makes even that answer non-productive and uncommunicative. 'Doubling up' on questions comes across as aggressive and pressuring, even if that is not the intention. Remember, communication is as much about perception as it is the meaning of the actual words.

But more than that, research at the University of Minnesota shows that adolescents and teenagers—due to the fact that their 'neural circuitry' is still in a state of flux—are, under most circumstances, poor at multi-tasking. The neural connections between brain-cells—especially in the frontal cortex—are not sufficiently refined to process large amounts of information coming in simultaneously and demanding conscious attention. So, pressing them to focus on different aspects of a problem simultaneously can produce an internal tension, resulting in frustration and, on occasions, an almost involuntary anger reaction.

As the leader of the Minnesota study, Professor Monica Luciana said, '*We need to keep their limitations in mind, especially when adolescents are confronted with demanding situations in the classroom, at home, or in social gatherings.*' [31]

This is why teenagers will often react in an inappropriate and extreme manner, to what appears to be a quite reasonable request—if that request happens to be made while they are concentrating on something else. It's nothing personal, and it's not intentional. It's just what happens when the subconscious sense of 'overload' triggers a response in the young person's hyper-reactive amygdala (the 'non-conscious' seat of our reactive emotions).

When asking questions, we will elicit information better one point at a time.

Interrupting or Anticipating Answers:

If we do either of these things, we may be wrong, and even if we are right it will be disempowering for the young person. If you have asked the question, have the courtesy to listen to the answer before commenting.

Derailing the young person's train of thought has the same effect as multiple questions—it forces them to consider more than one concept simultaneously, and can create the overload effect referred to above. The last thing we need when trying to get to the heart of an issue is that kind of unnecessary tension.

GOLDEN RULE NUMBER TWO: GIVE YOUR FULL ATTENTION TO ALL THE POSSIBILITIES IN A COMMUNICATION SITUATION—NO MATTER WHAT THE DISTRACTIONS

When we wish to really communicate with a child/teenager, or when they really want to communicate with us, it is a good idea to:

i)   Pay attention to the conversation and to the child as an important individual.

ii) Be free with hugs and other tactile signs of affection.

iii) Teach ourselves to smile.

iv) Understand the power of the right words to bolster self-esteem.

v)   Be willing to laugh at ourselves and admit when we have made a mistake.

vi) Maintain a sense of privacy between adult and child.

Confidence is the key to success—in exams and in every other area of life. The best way for a parent to build the confidence of a young person is to show respect—to acknowledge that they are important and that what they have to say is important. We cannot hope to guide or inspire if our children think we do not care, or that their concerns are not important enough to warrant our total attention.

Whether we are communicating face-to-face, or whether we just wish our child to know how we feel about them, focusing on all manner of communication modes is the key to effective inspiration.

Paying Attention:

If you are reading or watching TV, or if you have brought work home with you, stop and make it obvious that you are stopping willingly to talk about something 'more important'. Communication is primarily an emotional activity. Until the young person feels that his/her ideas, problems or concerns are of emotional significance to you, he/she will either not share them fully, or not assign the value to your responses that they properly deserve.

By stopping what we are doing, and giving the young person our full attention, we give the right emotional signal to open up strong communication channels.

If you are cooking, or doing something the young person can help with, it is sometimes good to talk as you work together. This builds rapport and makes him/her feel involved and important. You will be able to judge whether this is the appropriate approach—and often this will depend on the emotional content of the matter under discussion.

If it is not the best time to talk at the moment your child approaches you, it is important that they understand that it is no reflection on their importance, but simply a result of circumstances. Following up on the conversation as soon as possible afterwards reassures the child, and shows that you respect them and their issues.

The Power of Touch:

Children and even teenagers are often very kinaesthetic. A touch or a hug can communicate as much positive emotion as a thousand well-chosen words.

For many parents in many cultures, the power of the human touch has been played down—even discouraged—but it is a natural part of communication, dating back to our earliest ancestors. If we can overcome our learned behaviours and trust in what science has discovered about the power of touch, we can go a long way towards building a stronger, more supportive relationship with our children.

According to neuropsychologist James W. Prescott, *'Societies that provide infants with a great deal of physical affection ('tender loving care')'* [32] tend to produce relatively non-violent adults. On the other hand, the incidence of adult violence is significantly higher in societies in which children are rarely shown any tactile affection. This seems to be due to the fact that *'pleasure and violence have a reciprocal relationship, that is, the presence of one inhibits the other.'* [33]

While words and facial expressions are easily misinterpreted by the young—and especially by adolescents and teenagers—the meaning of a touch is generally unambiguous. A hand laid softly on the arm or the shoulder; the backs of the fingers touching or running softly down the cheek; a protective hug in times of high emotion—these are almost universally effective gestures of love and support, even in families which traditionally have not employed them.

A particularly effective gesture is to hold the child's gaze, while taking his/her head gently in both hands and drawing the child towards you, until your foreheads meet.

The Maori people of New Zealand do this as a loving greeting—foreheads and noses touch, and eye contact is maintained. It is called a '*hongi*'. The Inuit people (Eskimos) rub noses in a similar greeting.

One common symptom of dysfunctionality within a family is the inability of family members to display warmth and affection through tactile displays.

Smiling:

Most people underestimate the power of a smile to open up the channels of communication—even with total strangers. How much more effective is it likely to be when applied to someone we actually love? A smile banishes fear or insecurity, and says, 'I am here for you. Nothing you have to say can change the way I feel about you.'

And we all know how to smile, right? Everyone knows how to smile—even newborn babies. The thing is, newborns learn it because they are intimately in tune with the instinctive response it evokes in their parents and carers. It is a human survival mechanism; a genuine smile evokes a positive emotional response in the limbic system of the person receiving the smile, as automatically as the sight of a spider or a snake evokes the 'fight or flight' response.

Unfortunately, as we grow, many of us lose the innate ability to employ a smile to its greatest effect. Sometimes it is our socialisation—we are often (especially men) actively discouraged from showing 'soft' emotions. So, when we think it's time to smile—say for a formal photo, when the photographer is taking forever to focus the camera—the result is a bending of the lips that has little or no effect on the rest of the face.

This 'false' or forced smile—sometimes called the 'Miss Universe' smile—does not have the same effect on the recipient. In fact, it often prompts a negative, wary response, as the limbic system (our non-conscious 'emotion-centre') is particularly adept at reading the subtle nuances of expression that form the bulk of our non-verbal communications.

The good news is that if you have trouble with this particular area of communication, you can, without much effort, retrain yourself to smile. Use a mirror to practice maintaining eye contact—not always an accustomed behaviour in many parent-child relationships. In particular, practice smiling (not a grin, but a gentle, supportive softening of the features), so that you are accustomed to what it feels like when it is happening.

The best way to practice this is to tie it to an appropriate memory—a moment of genuine happiness or pride relating to your family. This will encourage a genuine smile—called a Duchenne smile, because it was first described by its discoverer, Guillame Duchenne. The key characteristic of a Duchenne smile is that it makes it up as far as the eyes.

Like an athlete training muscle response (sometimes called 'muscle-memory'), we need to be able to slip effectively into a supportive expression under sometimes very trying situations. Developing a muscle-memory for this very important expression is a highly advantageous strategy.

And it will not appear false. Remember, our driving motivation, even in times of stress is—or should be—our love and concern for our child. If this is not your driving emotion, then there will be no incentive to smile anyway.

Besides, there is strong evidence to suggest that the very act of smiling at someone has the effect of changing our own brain chemistry, so that the emotion more closely matches the expression.

The Right Words:
Sometimes, there is too much to say face-to-face for the way we feel to get a fair run. Tell your child she is remarkable. Say you love him. Occasionally, write personal messages to a young person which aren't 'To Do' lists.

Perhaps, each month, you could write a short letter (or a poem if you are feeling artistic) expressing what has made you particularly proud of your child in the past few weeks. Leave it on their bed, and don't mention it again. They may not mention it either—teens especially can be shy of talking about an overt demonstration of love—at least at first. Even if they don't acknowledge it, however, be assured. It will be treasured and it will certainly bolster their self-esteem.

Take the time to acknowledge their successes, commiserate with their setbacks, and voice your appreciation for little things. Discuss their interests, their music, and try to set aside your own likes, dislikes and personal prejudices.

You never know, you might learn to appreciate the melodic subtleties of heavy metal, the allure of the latest fashion statement or the athletic artistry of the latest dance moves. Even if you don't, showing that you are interested in understanding—that you are open to what your child regards as important—is the quickest way of strengthening an adult/child relationship.

Remember, however, that the interest must be genuine; young people can pick a fake, and it comes across as patronising.

Laughing at Ourselves:

There is no crime in being fallible and setting ourselves up as infallible is an impossible ideal to maintain.

Everyone makes mistakes—no one knows everything about everything—so accept the fact that you will end up from time to time with egg on your face, or a glaring error in your logic, and get over it.

When you 'drop the ball', own up to it, discuss it if necessary, and, if possible, laugh about it with your children. If you have seen your mistake, chances are they have seen it too, so you can only strengthen your position by being confident enough to admit it.

They, in turn, will be more likely to admit their error next time—and accept suggestions on how to fix it—if they are modelling on your example, and it will be far less damaging to their own fragile self-image if it is seen as a natural part of being human.

Keeping Conversations Private:

The best time for communication between parent and child is when no one else is around. We should only involve other parties if there is some specific reason why they need to be involved. Young people feel less pressured one-on-one.

Of course, this need for privacy extends beyond the conversation itself. Unless it is agreed during the discussion that the contents can be shared with a third party, then the rule should be that the contents of the conversation should be regarded as confidential. This gives the child confidence to share and teaches social responsibility—because the 'confidentiality clause' applies to both parties.

There will be times, of course, when this 'confidentiality clause' may need to be broken. If there is some compelling reason for this, then—as a matter of respect and to maintain the highest level of trust—it is important to let the child know first. Explain the reasons and discuss the consequences of not revealing the information to the other party.

Even if the child/teen is unhappy about the revelation, there is far less chance of long-term damage to your intimate relationship than if the decision is taken without any consultation.

GOLDEN RULE NUMBER THREE: BALANCE PRAISE AND CRITICISM—PROVIDE SUPPORT WHILE ENCOURAGING INDEPENDENCE

When assessing a child's/teenager's performance or achievement or when dealing with challenges, we should:

i)   Show that we will help if they really need you to, but not offer or try to solve every problem for them immediately.

ii) Use 'descriptive praise' that emphasises the positives and let the child know that we appreciate the effort when he/she is doing something well.

iii) Use 'I statements' ('I feel...', 'I think...'), rather than 'You statements' ('You always...' 'You are...' 'You should have...'), when giving criticism, and make
the criticism constructive, offering suggestions for how things might be done
better, rather than dwelling on the negatives.

iv) 'Gradually introduce' responsibility to our children.

'Empowerment' does not mean doing everything for a child—it means giving the young person the guidance and the confidence to back his/her own judgment. It is an important part of preparing a young person for the demands of the world—both during, and beyond, the school period. The more our children come to rely on us, the less able they will be to rely on themselves.

Guidance—Not Dependence:

When presented with a challenge facing our child—be it of an academic or a personal nature—it is by far the easiest approach to use our experience to create a solution, which can then be given fully-fledged to the young person. Problem solved.

If we know an answer, the quickest and least demanding response is to provide it, so that things can move efficiently onward.

If we see our child making a mistake, it is natural to 'set him/her straight' immediately—even forcefully—to avoid the inconvenience/embarrassment/extra work that repetition of the mistake might produce.

But is it the best approach?

> *Remember: The role of the parent is that of guide—not oracle, dictator or fairy godmother.*

If a young person never has to solve problems or deal with adversity, how can they learn how to react to such events, when you are no longer there to solve everything for them?

This is the problem with having a tutor 'on tap'. The child becomes a 'dependent learner'—dependent on someone else's knowledge and skill to solve problems.

Praise and help are good, but rather than constantly emphasising—and ensuring—successes, we can help our children develop and maintain a healthy self-image by helping them cope with defeats as well.

During times of disappointment or crisis, let your children know that you still love and support them, no matter the result. Do this, and failures will not assume such a world-swallowing importance.

The research of Professor Allan Snyder indicates that being able to cope with and embrace the learnings provided by setbacks and adversity is one of the key markers of championship. Naturally, our support during the process is great for a child's morale.

In *What Makes a Champion!*, Professor Snyder writes:

> *'Champions are often familiar with adversity. They have had to 'fight' to get where they are… They learn how to convert… 'upsets into set-ups'… Struggling in the early learning process possibly acclimatises us to difficulties, and may advantage us in dealing with adversity [later].*
>
> *'What has emerged from our research is the possible necessity of*

overcoming adversity as a preparation for being a champion.' [34]

Show that you will help if he/she needs you to, but don't offer or try to solve every problem for a young person immediately. If we can use our experience to help children to ask 'proactive' questions (that is, questions which help clarify the issue, and/or open the mind and set the non-conscious 'search-engine' looking for possible solutions), we empower them for individual decision-making and action in the future.

The Use of 'Descriptive Praise':

If the young person has gone to some effort to do a job well, we should go to a little more effort in recognising the particulars of that effort. Descriptive praise means that we are paying attention—and for most young people, that is a reward in itself.

> *'Greg, this story is sensational. I love the way you've made Daisy come to life—I really feel I know her. Did you mean for the reader to feel sorry for Lance? Because I really did. By the way, how was your Maths homework today? Anything you want to talk about?'*

is much better than

> *'That's great, Greg. Now, did you do your Maths homework, or are you going to rush it again in the morning, as usual?'*

Parental approval is a significant motivator in people of all ages, and descriptive praise implies genuine approval.

- It is not off-hand or automatic.
- It acknowledges effort, recognises particular examples of ingenuity or creative problem-solving.
- It has the effect of positively reinforcing the extra thought or effort that has been put into accomplishing a (sometimes) everyday task.

The feeling of achievement that such recognition evokes will encourage a willingness to earn more appreciation in the future. This is because the emotional 'reward' of our recognition is tied at a non-conscious level to the action itself, creating an anchor for (and therefore likely repetition of) the behaviour.

Using 'Constructive Criticism'—'I' Statements Rather Than 'You' Statements:
There is a subtle difference between using an 'I' statement (I really feel that...), and a 'you' statement (You have caused 'X' to happen, because...). An 'I' statement focuses the young person on the effect a behaviour/situation/piece of writing etc. has had on us, whereas a 'you' statement comes across as a criticism of the person, rather than the action.

> *'I would really like it if you could spend some time tidying your room this weekend. It saves me a whole lot of time vacuuming if the clothes have been put in the wash and I've got a clear floor to work with,'*

works a whole lot better than

> *'Your room is a pig-sty. How can you live like this? If you don't tidy it up by Saturday, I'll...'*

He can 'live like this' because his priorities (especially if he is a teenager) are elsewhere. He simply doesn't notice the mess the way you do. If he has a positive reason to notice it (i.e. it will make you happier and cause him less 'hassle') then you may well achieve the desired result.

Threats will tend to harden his resolve—especially if he does not see the 'mess' as a problem in the first place. If you make it a problem, then it is your problem, and though he might accede to your 'demands', it will be with some reluctance.

Introducing Responsibility 'Step by Step':
By assuming accountability one small step at a time, young people learn to develop responsible attitudes. They feel more useful and valued, and invariably respond positively. To learn social responsibility, they need to practice being responsible.

Our example is important, of course, but we wouldn't expect our child to learn to drive just by watching us. Observation gives them the basic principles—the driving instincts—but they need to sit behind the wheel and get a feel for the gears, the brakes and the steering—the 'muscle-memory' for the complex act of driving—if they are ever going to become accomplished drivers.

Responsibility, like driving, is a hands-on skill.

GOLDEN RULE NUMBER FOUR: DEVELOP STRATEGIES FOR CONTROLLING THE NEGATIVE EMOTION IN ANY SITUATION

When emotions (ours or the young person's) threaten to get in the way of solving a conflict situation, it is important to have response strategies in place to defuse the moment. We should:

i) Always try to understand the young person's reason for committing some 'unacceptable' behaviour.

ii) Develop strategies to avoid 'standing over' a child.

iii) Use a 'time-out' to regain emotional control.

iv) Find alternatives to the 'why' question by reframing it as a 'how' or 'what' question.

v) Develop strategies for preventing—or dealing with—lying.

vi) Learn to create effective questions—and consider the power (and danger) of the ill-considered question.

No two people—especially parents and children—have the same perspective on any situation. Understanding this basic truth is the first step to being able to avoid—or control—the negative emotions which will inevitably develop at times when those different perspectives come into conflict.

Though conflicting perspectives may be inevitable, and though we may at times be hurt, disappointed or angry at the way things have developed, we must be aware of our responsibility, as the mature party, to find solutions to the impasse— to control the emotion and engineer a positive result.

Understanding the Different Perspectives:

It is important to remember that, very often, a young person's reason for committing some 'unacceptable' behaviour may be perfectly logical and acceptable—or even necessary—from his/her inexperienced or limited perspective.

Before overreacting, I need to be sure that we are both talking about the same incident, and remind myself that his/her 'camera angle' and mine might be radically different—for very good reasons. If I approach the incident in a calm, supportive manner, rather than an accusatory one, I stand a good chance of understanding the motivation behind the action—which might never come out if the situation spirals into confrontation.

For an excellent example of this process in action, watch the very moving sequence in the Ron Howard film *Cinderella Man* (2005) where James Braddock, an impoverished but loving Depression-era father, deals with the fact that his son has stolen meat from the local butcher's shop.

After returning the stolen meat, Braddock does not immediately demand an explanation. He has already registered his disappointment (and his authority) and redressed the 'public' aspect of the situation, so the 'social' lesson has been learned. Now, he waits until the child has thought things through, and offered his explanation—which was that other children in the area had been forced to leave their struggling families to stay with people who could feed them.

At this point, understanding the child's fear and seeing the action as an immature attempt to ward off a far greater 'evil', Braddock shows his respect for the child—without condoning the action—by crouching in front of the boy (bringing himself to the same level), and seriously addressing the very real fear that drove the behaviour in the first place.

Braddock reassures the child by promising that, no matter how bad things get, they will never be separated—removing the emotional cause of the child's unacceptable behaviour.

Only then does he remind the boy that no matter what the circumstances, 'We never take what isn't ours.'

Would that we all had that sort of relationship with our children!

This sequence suggests a four-point checklist for defusing an explosive situation:

1. If necessary, resolve the 'public' situation first. As long as others are involved, it is more difficult to get to the truth, as the emotional 'interference' is too distracting.
2. Give the child time to consider the situation without confrontation.
3. Take steps to get to the 'real story'—the intent or influence behind the action. From an ethical stand-point, the intention is often more important than the actual action.
4. Resolve the situation in consultation with the child. Imposed decisions are rarely satisfactory—for either party—in the long run.

Especially in times of crisis, or when they might feel that they are in trouble, don't 'stand over' your child:

Posture, as we will see later, is a key indicator of the relative 'power' of individuals in any situation. Physically, try to get down to the young person's level (crouch, sit on a low stool or on the floor) then talk. For an excellent example of this approach, watch a really good Kindergarten teacher in operation.

If a teenager is sitting or lying on the lounge or the bed, sit down next to them before commencing. Even if you are both standing, sitting down first changes the dynamic, easing some of the tension. Sharing a drink or food can also help. The idea is to remove the 'power-differential' barrier and open up the channels of communication.

If you are very angry about a behaviour or an incident, allow some 'time out' to calm yourself and regain control before dealing with the incident:

Almost two thousand years ago, the Roman orator and playwright Seneca wrote, 'The greatest remedy for anger is delay.' [35] He understood that emotional responses are rarely as effective as considered ones.

Though I might feel the need to address the incident immediately, it is far better to deal with it effectively and with a positive resolution, than simply to satisfy the momentary emotional urge and suffer the unforeseen consequences.

Remember the anonymous comedian's sage advice: 'The early bird might well get the worm, but it is the second mouse that gets the cheese.'

A better approach is to send the child away on his or her own, to think about what has occurred, then find a way to disperse the anger before discussing the incident. This will allow for better communication, and it will also allow time for the child to reflect on the behaviour in question.

Many of a young person's actions are taken on the spur of the moment, but immediate confrontation—before they have had the opportunity to consider the unforeseen effects of those actions—forces them into a position of defending their behaviour.

With the non-conscious working overtime, to deal with the perceived threat, they will be able, under pressure, to find some kind of justification. This then becomes a part of their defensive position in the conflict situation, muddying the waters and making resolution of the situation all the more difficult.

'Time-out' before any discussion gives the child time to consider the situation without having to defend the indefensible to another party.

My distress, disappointment and/or anger will already have registered through my demeanour and body language (more about this below). As a result, the child's non-conscious—tuned as it is to the important clues in its environment—will be working overtime to analyse the 'cause and effect' relationship between the action and my reaction.

The child is forced, by this process, to consider elements that were not considered at the time of the action. This is the beginning of an understanding of my perspective on the situation—which opens the door to better communication when, calm and under control, I finally initiate the discussion.

Avoiding the 'Why?' Question:
We don't ask 'Why?' as our first question. 'Why?' is usually interpreted as an accusation demanding an excuse, and puts the child on the defensive. It is far better to begin by simply asking the child *what* happened. The 'why' will follow naturally, but without 'forcing' the justification—which may be cloudy at best.

Alternatively, we could use phrases like: 'tell me all you can', or 'what were your feelings?' Questions which draw out the truth without accusation reduce the level of threat the child is feeling and lead to a resolution far more efficiently than threats and badgering.

> *The child's primary need is to feel loved and accepted. If telling the truth is what achieves that result, then the truth becomes the preferred option.*

Badgering a child to get to the truth is counter-productive. Eventually he/she will break and we will 'win', but at what cost? We have not discouraged lying—if we have asked the child ten times before receiving the truth, then we have given him ten opportunities to practice telling lies, and we have become progressively more angry and threatening in the process.

When the child finally 'breaks', the lesson he has learned from the ordeal is not, *'Lying doesn't pay,'* but rather, *'If I'm going to avoid this ordeal again, I need to learn to become a better liar.'* If we show that we still accept and love the child regardless of what he has or has not done, we reduce the 'need' for lying.

Sanctions which are fair—and preferably negotiated—combined with an attitude that shows the child that he is still loved, in spite of there being a necessary consequence to the behaviour, gives the young person a sense of security and structure. This makes the punishment acceptable and 'positive', and reduces the tendency to lie in the future.

Dealing with the Lie:

If a child is lying, or likely to tell a lie, and we have prior knowledge of the situation, the best approach is to inform the child that we have information on the incident and ask her to think for a few minutes about what occurred before revealing what really happened.

The truth at that point will be a preferable option, and we will be free to deal with the original incident, instead of adding the 'crime' of lying to the mix. We should never try to use information to trap a child in a lie. Rather, we should accept the fact that human beings lie—especially if they are inexperienced children with underdeveloped frontal lobes, and an incomplete notion of cause and effect.

Their real desire is to end the situation without getting into trouble. We are interested in getting to the truth and finding ways to resolve the issue—not in scoring cheap points in an imaginary competition. The key to preventing lying in children and teenagers is to be consistent in the strategies we employ to deal with incidents—and with lies.

Creating Effective Questions:

It is important to remember that questions have the power to dictate the direction of the conversation. We have to be careful, therefore, that the question we ask is leading in the direction we wish to go.

If Rebecca has left her shoes in the hallway—again!—one of the favourite questions that parents might ask is, *'Who left these shoes in the hallway?'* to which the reply comes, *'I did.'* and the shoes stay right there.

The question was actually a sarcastic request for the shoes to be moved, but the child/teen has chosen to answer it literally as a request for information. Younger children are literal by nature, and teens often choose to be literal as a form of 'passive resistance' to authority.

An old saying warns that 'sarcasm is the lowest form of wit'. It is also the lowest form of communication, because it serves no other purpose than to antagonise—which is why it has also been called 'a stupid way of being clever'.

While many sarcastic remarks are superficially clever in an intellectual sense, they show little emotional intelligence—and it is emotional intelligence which decides our level of success in all relationships.

Psychologically, sarcasm communicates contempt, and research into the breakdown of marriages suggests that—more than anger, or disappointment—evidence of contempt on the part of one or both of the partners is the strongest predictor of eventual divorce.

If this is the case between married couples, why should it be any different between parents (or teachers) and children?

The trick is not to allow the situation to develop in the first place. If I follow up my first question with, 'Why do you always leave your shoes in the hallway?' [Real meaning: 'I'm tired of picking up after you.'] I am opening myself up to further frustration, as the young person replies, 'You don't want me to get dirt on the carpet, do you?'

I have effectively allowed the child to justify the action—in terms of my needs—instead of resolving the situation, and now I have to 'assert my authority' in a more aggressive and confrontational manner than would have been necessary had I said what I really meant from the beginning.

If you want the shoes moved, then simply ask her to move them—politely, but with authority. 'Rebecca, put your shoes away in the cupboard, please. Now.' There is no ambiguity and she cannot shift the responsibility, so she is far more likely to accede without resistance.

Good communication is the life-blood of change and growth for your child, and—especially at times of high stress—it may be just the transfusion he/ she needs.

2. How to Establish and Maintain an Emotional 'Connection'

'The only fault's with time. All men become good creatures: but so slow!' [36]

Robert Browning

Non-Verbal Communication—'The Lion's Share'

The word 'communication' comes from the Old French word, *'comuner'*, meaning 'common'. When we communicate, we share something in common—information, emotion, meaning. We cannot communicate alone and we cannot (unless we have some very specific types of psychosis) communicate with an inanimate object.

Communication is far more than simply taking it in turns to talk. It is a two-way street, a cycle in which each party influences the response of the other party and is in turn influenced by that response. It is useful to remember, therefore, that both parties can be regarded as wholly responsible for whatever communication takes place.

We cannot argue, *'I meant X, but she misinterpreted it.'* The ultimate meaning of anything we say is the meaning that the other party takes from it. What I intended—what I meant—is, in the end, irrelevant to the outcome. Even not saying anything and keeping still communicates something, and it is pointless to protest, *'I didn't say anything.'*

How carefully do we choose the words we use in a conversation with our children?

We have already examined the nature of questions and the effects of positive and negative statements—the content of our conversation—but, it is instructive to remember what the old Jewish proverb advises:

'A mother understands what her child does not say.'

An insightful comment on parenthood to be sure, but, significantly, the reverse is also true. What we don't say accounts for an important part of what we communicate to our children.

Would it surprise you to learn that according to well-respected international research, only around seven per cent of the meaning in any conversation is carried by the words we choose?

Seven per cent... So, what is doing the communicating for us?

The pitch, speed, quality and volume of our voice—what we call the tonality—contributes approximately 38 per cent. The other 55 per cent (over half of our communication) comes from our physiology—that is, our posture, gestures, facial expressions (including how often we blink) and our breathing.

In an earlier discussion of teenage behaviour, we referred to fMRI studies comparing teenage and adult brains engaged in identifying emotions from photographs. These studies showed that due to the immaturity of their pre-frontal lobes, adolescents tended to respond emotionally, rather than applying the more 'rational' processes of the frontal cortex. The result was that they were much more likely to misinterpret facial expressions and make incorrect judgments about the emotions of others than adults were.

Relating this research to teenage driving habits, Katherine Cheng, in her paper 'Confessions of a Teenage Mind', has this to say about teenage driving behaviours.

> 'It is reasonable to speculate that teenagers are frequently involved in car collisions because they misinterpret the behaviours of other drivers as threatening and therefore drive more aggressively, or perhaps some drive more recklessly because they do not fully think through the consequences of their decisions, particularly in high-stress driving conditions.' [37]

Clearly, these studies have a significant bearing on discussions relating to the appropriate minimum age for driving, drinking—and even for military conscription.

What we are particularly interested in here, however, is the effect of the young person's misinterpretation of visual clues on your ability to achieve successful communication—especially in tense situations.

Given the young person's tendency to misinterpret the meaning of facial expressions and other 'clues' to meaning, the relative importance of posture and facial expressions in determining what is communicated is significant.

With the lion's share (93 per cent) of our communication relying on the interpretation of non-verbal cues, the likelihood of a young person misunderstanding the meaning and intent of our words is extremely high. This is especially true if the situation is already emotional, or if the young person is already feeling insecure.

Consider this example:

> Your daughter, sixteen, comes in dressed for an important night out. It is vital to her that she makes a good impression, and she values your opinion, so as she enters she asks, 'How do I look?' You glance up and say, 'Beautiful.'

All things being equal, she should be pleased with your response, but what if that single word was delivered with a rolling of the eyes, a slight curl of the lip and a sarcastic, dismissive tone in the voice? The tone of your voice and your body language conspire, under such circumstances, to radically change the meaning of that single word, tearing down the young girl's fragile self-esteem.

Of course, you would never be so cruel or uncaring intentionally, but perhaps at that moment, you are a little worried about the household budget or something at work, or a week of long hours has tired you. As a result, the expression on your face is not a precise match with the message you wish to convey.

To an emotionally vulnerable teenager, the unsmiling face—or the duller than anticipated tone of voice—might alter the intended meaning significantly.

Even if you didn't mean it to.

Remember: *The real meaning of the communication is the reaction that you get...*

Conversation Management Strategies

Understanding the danger, however, helps us to manage the situation more effectively. It means that we should learn to pay as much attention to *how* we say things as we do to the words we choose. We have already seen how the decision to avoid standing over a child creates a better emotional connection, but there are many other ways in which we can defuse a potential confrontation or upset.

Observing the Visual Clues

One way is to be particularly observant of the young person's immediate response to anything we say. Being better than they are at reading visual clues, we should be able to pick if anything we have said has been misunderstood, simply by watching the young person's reaction.

If a statement or facial expression has been misinterpreted as aggressive, hurtful or angry—a common mistake, as discussed previously—we can correct the mistake immediately. Start by making a statement such as, '*I mean it, Tahlia, really. You look fabulous...*'

Follow this with a piece of descriptive praise, like, '*That colour really brings out the brown in your eyes,*' or '*I wish I looked that good in a pair of jeans,*' delivered in a consciously more enthusiastic tone.

What we *don't* say is, '*What's the matter?*'

This question focuses the child on the emotion she is feeling, an emotion she may be trying hard to hide, embarrassing her and making her feel even worse. It is also likely to be interpreted as a challenge—as you defending your earlier criticism—thus reinforcing the impression that your original response created.

Remember Golden Rule Number Two: It is important to show you are genuinely interested and to give her your full attention—even if you have issues of your own. They are not her issues, and allowing them to overflow into your relationship with her makes things more difficult for everyone.

Tonality

Just as young people misinterpret facial expressions, they also interpret increased volume or higher pitch as aggressive or angry. If you sense a growing tension and there is no obvious reason for it in what you have said (or intended to say), one of the tricks to keeping negative emotion out of the discussion is to consciously speak slowly at a lower pitch and volume.

Explaining Your Feelings

As a general rule, you can train your child to better read your body language and tonality by simply explaining how you feel: *'I'm not angry, Suzie, but I am disappointed…'* or *'I understand why you thought you had to do it, Aidan, but you must understand that it worries me…'*

If the child asks, *'Why are you angry?'* hold his/her gaze gently and reply with something like, *'Look at my face, Angela. Do I really look angry? This is worry/ concern/ fear/confusion'* (or whatever the emotion is that you are feeling). Such a reply should be accompanied by a gentle touch to indicate you are not frustrated or angered by the youngster's misinterpretation of your feelings.

For a superb example of this approach in action, look at the scenes in M. Night Shyamalan's movie *The Sixth Sense*, where young Cole Sears' mother (played impeccably by Toni Collette) strives—under the most extreme conditions imaginable—to reassure her distressed son that she still loves and supports him.

Her strategy is to break the emotional pre-occupation, by directing his attention to her face so that she can hold his gaze and explain the emotion she is feeling, in words and gestures which he will understand and respond to.

What's in a Name..?

Notice, that all of the replies suggested above incorporate the child's name.

Our own name is an essential part of our identity. In fact, it has been called 'the most beautiful sound in the world'. Spoken gently, with love, especially by a parent or lover, and especially when it is accompanied by a gentle touch on the hand or the cheek, it has a comforting and reassuring effect on us—soothing us more than a thousand carefully chosen words, and demonstrating acceptance of who we are.

Below are more strategies to aid in building emotional connection—an essential skill, as true communication can only take place once a rapport is established.

Other Connection-Building Strategies:

Breathing

Carefully observing a person's breathing, and bringing our own breathing pattern into rhythm with it is an extremely effective method of connecting at a non-conscious level. Understanding this is very valuable when dealing with young people, because once connection has been established, gradually changing your own breathing pattern, slowing it down, can induce the young person to follow our lead unconsciously and slow their own breathing.

The relationship between breathing rate and emotional state is very strong. If someone is upset, they will tend to breathe more quickly, taking short, shallow breaths. Slowing the breathing down and deepening it has a calming effect, which might become significant in certain situations.

The Simple Act of Nodding

Another important 'connecting' strategy is one of the oldest and most universally used gestures. When listening to what the young person has to say, gently nod your head up and down. This has two extremely important effects.

Firstly, it is a physical demonstration that you are paying attention. It communicates acceptance, and encourages the young person to continue sharing. It does not necessarily imply that you agree with everything that is being said, but if, later, you choose to question one or two elements of the child's position, the simple fact that you have nodded acceptance of the child's right to speak means that the later criticism or query is isolated, as it should be, to the particular point you are making. It does not negate automatically, everything the child has said.

Secondly, (as revealed by recent research by Richard Petty and Pablo Briñol, at the Universidad Autonoma de Madrid in Spain), the very act of nodding my head acts physiologically on my brain, making me more confident to trust my own judgment in relation to the information in question.

The Petty/Briñol study concluded that nodding your head up and down has the effect of actually reinforcing the feeling that you have confidence in your own thoughts. And it doesn't matter if those thoughts are positive or negative.

Shaking your head does the opposite: it gives you less confidence in your own judgments.

This means that as well as making the young person more comfortable while sharing their thoughts, thus giving me a better insight into their perspective, the simple physical act of nodding affects my own input to the situation. By raising my confidence level, it also encourages my non-conscious to seek out positive responses with greater self-assurance, and this confident attitude will inevitably communicate itself to the child.

Show your children you're proud of them. The child within us all needs to know that our parents are proud of us and believe in us.

HOW TO APPLY THE KNOWLEDGE

These exercises are all designed to support our development as a communicator. How often—and with how much enthusiasm—we practice our communication skills will determine the effect we can have on our child's 'champion mindset'.

EXERCISE 1. COMMUNICATION STOCKTAKE

From time to time—and more frequently, at first, while the process is being reinforced—it is a useful discipline to take stock of our success in applying the Four Golden Rules of Communication.

Choose one of the Rules, and do a quick, informal stocktake—it helps to build awareness of our communication style; to keep the strategies in the forefront of the mind.

Rule #1: Awareness of Processing Limitations

Key Strategies:

i) Ask just one question at a time.

ii) Allow the young person to finish speaking, instead of attempting to anticipate his/her answers.

iii) Avoid the temptation to interrupt his/her answers, even if the words suggest a response.

Action:

Write down at least three times during the past three days when you have:

i) Forgotten to apply one of the Key Strategies

—What was the result?

—Did you remedy the situation? If so, how? What was the effect?

ii) Remember to apply one of the Key Strategies

—What was the result?

—How did you feel? Was communication easier?

Rule #2: Giving Your Full Attention—Avoiding Distractions

Key Strategies:

i) Pay attention to the conversation and to your child as an important individual.

ii) Be free with hugs and other tactile signs of affection.

iii) Teach yourself to smile.

iv) Understand the power of the right words to bolster self-esteem.

v) Be willing to laugh at yourself and admit when you have made a mistake.

vi) Maintain a sense of privacy between you and your child.

Action:

Consider the past three days:

i) On a scale from 1–10, rate your performance on each of the Key Stategies.

—What did you do that you are particularly proud of? Which areas need more work?

Rule #3: Balancing Praise and Criticism

Key Strategies:

i) Be there for them—but only where necessary.

ii) Use 'descriptive praise'.

iii) Use 'I' statements.

iv) 'Gradually introduce' responsibility.

Action:

Consider the past three days:

i) On a scale from 1–10, rate your performance on each of the Key Stategies.

—What did you do that you are particularly proud of? Which areas need more work?

Rule #4: Controlling Negative Emotion

Key Strategies:

i) Understand the reasons for a given behaviour.

ii) Avoid 'standing over' your child.

iii) Use a 'time out'.

iv) Find 'how' or 'what' alternatives to the 'why' question.

v) Deal positively with lying.

vi) Choose questions carefully.

Action:

Consider the past three days:

i) Pick three occasions which involved some level of negative emotion.

—How did you try to control the emotion?

—How did your strategy work?

—What did you learn from the process? Would you use the same approach again? Why / why not?

EXERCISE 2. MAKING CHANGES

At the start of Part Two, we quoted Karl Jung. He related the changes we desire in our children to changes that we might need to make in ourselves. As with most of his observations, Jung's advice is sound—if difficult to live up to.

We have to assume that whatever we do or say will act as a model for our children's behaviour. But much of our behaviour is habitual—which is to say that we don't always think about what we are doing, or about the effect it may have on a young person's impressionable mind.

The following approach helps us to put our own behaviour in perspective. It can be done alone—or preferably both parents can do it together.

A. If, as a parent or teacher, you are alone:

i) Write down on a piece of paper anything that you consistently do or say which you would not want your child(ren) to imitate.

ii) Once you have your list, write down next to each entry an alternative (preferable) behaviour—one that you would like to be the model for your child(ren) to follow.

The simple act of writing it down establishes it as a matter of importance, and this means that you will be more aware of your habitual behaviour from then on.

iii) When you find yourself saying or doing one of the things on the list, consciously shift to the alternative behaviour, so that it becomes the new 'habit'. This is called a 'conscious reframe', and it has the effect of strengthening (or 'habitualising') the new behaviour.

The most difficult part of this process comes when the old behaviour happens in front of the child.

iv) The best approach, under these circumstances is honesty. Shift into the conscious reframe as described above, but make sure that you explain that sometimes even parents/teachers have to correct themselves—and that this is the best way to behave in this situation.

A parent or teacher who is willing to correct bad habits in him/herself has far more credibility, when correcting the mistakes or behaviour of the child.

B. If, as parents, you are able to undertake the process together, the effect on your children will be far greater, and you will be able to support change in each other.

As a first step, work out together the behaviours which each of you needs to change. This should not be seen as a chance to tell each other all the things that 'bug' you about your partner's habits. There is no recrimination involved. Rather, it should be entered into as an opportunity to make a difference.

i) It should begin with each partner identifying his/her own 'bad habits'—which should surface most issues if both parties are being honest with themselves. Any key behaviours which have not been surfaced can then be added by the other party in a constructive and non-confrontational way. The agreement is that no offence will be taken, no matter what is brought up.

ii) Together, work on Step Two—the alternative behaviours list. Once this is done, then it is easy to work out strategies which will enable you to work together to make the necessary changes.

Of course, self-correction is best as a model, but if both parents are working together—and if it is done right—it is an opportunity to support each other.

Note: It is not good for one parent to be seen 'correcting' the behaviour of the other—a 'united-front' on the part of the parents provides young people with a greater sense of security.

Therefore:

iii) It is a good idea to develop a code-word or a specific action which acts as a 'circuit-breaker'—a warning of 'bad habit' behaviour, and a trigger for the alternative action. It is important that it be quite subtle—a phrase or gentle touch, that suggests support rather than correction, and a willingness on both parts to make the shift swiftly and without a negative reaction to the suggestion.

It is important also that the parent making the adjustment be the one to draw it to the child's attention, so that the message is one of self-correction, rather than 'policing'.

EXERCISE 3. HIGH-POINT/LOW-POINT

Everyone has high-points and low-points in their day. Sometimes, the high-points dominate and it is a good day, sometimes it is the low-points that dominate and the day is less than spectacular. A great communication strategy that can also become a family-building ritual takes place at the dinner table (or it can be adapted to create a one-on-one rapport-building exercise between teacher and student).

i) The parent picks a child, and asks, "High-point or Low-point?" This gives the child the chance to choose the most important element in their day to share. Choice is a key factor, as it can often surface what is truly important to the child.

ii) The child might say, "High-point. I got chosen for the swimming team." Or maybe, "Low-point. I got Maths detention for forgetting to do my homework."

iii) Either way, the topic is open for discussion—and the celebration or learning can follow.

Note: It is important that anything brought up in the 'High-point/Low-point' context—especially a 'Low-point'—is discussed without anger or recrimination or recourse to negative emotion. This is a long-term communication strategy, and angry, sarcastic or punitive responses will fatally undermine it.

Similarly, if the 'Low-point' is something seemingly beyond the child's control, the purpose of the exercise is not to wallow in a 'sympathetic' emotion, but to open the problem up for discussion, with a view to finding a workable solution.

The key is to keep the atmosphere light and supportive—both for the high-points and the low ones.

iv) Once the discussion exhausts itself, the person last chosen chooses the next participant, by asking, "High-point or Low-point?"—and parents are not exempt.

v) The sequence repeats until all family members have had a chance to share.

For a family to function effectively, there must be times when unfettered communication can take place, and the shared meal is an ideal opportunity. Eating in front of the TV or at different times and in different places is a lost opportunity for family-building.

It is amazing—and sad—how many parents know little or nothing about what happens during their child's day, and often, a parent's life beyond the home is a total mystery to the children. This is an activity that can change that situation—permanently.

part three

HOW TO CREATE AN EMOTIONALLY-BALANCED ENVIRONMENT

Abolishing Anger, Banishing Blame, Refining Responsibility—Seeking Solutions

---

'It is better to bind your children to you by a feeling of respect and by gentleness, than by fear.' [38]

TERENCE

ABOLISHING ANGER

BALANCING HEAD
AND HEART

REFINING
RESPONSIBILITY

BANISHING BLAME

THE ETHICAL
SPECTRUM

SEEKING
SOLUTIONS

*'If you want children to keep
their feet on the ground, put
some responsibility on their
shoulders.'* [41]

ABIGAIL VAN BUREN

An Emotionally-Balanced Environment

When we talk about an emotionally-balanced environment, the 'balance' we refer to is one between the 'first-response' emotions and the more considered, analytical and logical responses that we, as human beings, are capable of.

We have already seen that emotions are not the ideal tool for resolving the conflicts or challenges of everyday life. The use of logical or analytical thinking can be of great advantage in refining solutions or selecting appropriate responses.

Of course, being human, and having our embotions so intimately involved in all of our reactions to the world beyond ourselves, it is unrealistic to think that all problems or challenges can be solved purely through analysis and logic.

This is especially true when we are dealing with young people.

Even if it were possible to quarantine our emotions completely, almost inevitably we would appear 'cold and unfeeling' to another individual. This creates an instinctive resistance, making even an 'obvious and logical' solution unacceptable.

The answer is to first acknowledge—and validate—the emotions on both sides; to understand where they come from and the effect they may be having on individuals' reactions. Once the emotions have been identified, however, their influence must be balanced by a more structured thought process, so that we are not dominated by 'gut-responses'.

Formulated to deepen communication and discover workable solutions, the strategies outlined in Part Three are based on the strategy of embracing both sides of our human nature.

1. How to Abolish Anger

'Anger blows out the lamp of the mind. In the examination of a great and important question, everyone should be serene, slow-pulsed and calm.' [40]

Robert Green Ingersoll

Nobody is perfect—even with three or four decades (or more!) of experience under their belt.

If we accept the essential truth of this statement, we should be prepared to expect human failings in the young as part of the natural order of things—and as an acceptable everyday challenge.

Of course, the most effective way to deal with challenges is to create solutions. The least effective is to react emotionally—especially if the emotion of choice is anger.

Almost two and a half thousand years ago, writing on the subject of anger, Aristotle pointed out that:

> '*Anybody can become angry, that is easy; but to be angry with the right person, and to the right degree, and at the right time, and for the right purpose, and in the right way, that is not within everybody's power and is not easy.*' [41]

Without going into the more detailed biochemical and bioelectrical changes that anger produces within the brain, it suffices to say that the chance of maintaining the ability to think clearly and make effective choices is significantly reduced once anger alters the brain patterns. The angry brain shifts to a hyper-reactive state, releasing powerful chemicals into the blood-stream and the brain, which prepare the body for immediate—usually aggressive—physical action.

Very valuable in a situation of grave physical threat—not so useful when dealing with a confused or emotionally fragile child or teenager.

We have discussed previously the beneficial effect of removing the emotion from our response to a disagreement, and the use of proactive questions and the brainstorming process to achieve a compromise solution to an impasse. But what about deliberate bad behaviour, wilful disobedience, damage to valued possessions—even physical or emotional hurt? How negotiable can we afford to be under these circumstances? How do we keep the anger reaction out of the equation?

No one said that modern parenting was easy—or even natural. After all, we live in an environment which ceased to be 'natural' centuries ago.

This means that we need to develop responses which suit the environment into which we—and, more importantly, our children—were born, rather than relying on inbuilt reflexive and emotional responses, which evolved as 'hard-wired' survival strategies in a world far different from our own.

The threat of violence and the strength of the dominant male or female is enough to maintain order and obedience in most pack or herd animals—as it was in many primitive societies or tribal groups. After all, in many ways, our tribal and even our urban instincts are a throwback to our ancient ancestry—both human and primate—they are a part of our DNA.

In 21st Century society, however, any form of violence, physical or emotional, is a counter-productive strategy.

In the modern context, it is instructive to consider Indira Gandhi's beautifully ambiguous comment on compromise.

'*You cannot,*' she said, '*shake hands with a clenched fist.*' [42]

Training children in the values and behaviours necessary for living 'in close quarters' with thousands—or millions—of other individuals requires practice in a very different approach to modifying a child's behaviour.

> *Violence begets violence, and in an urban environment, teaching a child—through your example—that violence, or the threat of violence, is a viable solution to any dispute is to create a seriously dysfunctional future citizen.*

Earlier, we looked at the advantages of taking time to disperse the anger before attempting to communicate. This skill is absolutely essential for effective parenting. Remember Newton's Third Law—'*For every action, there is an equal and opposite reaction.*'

Newton, of course, was talking about the notion of Force in physics, but the same principle holds true of interpersonal forces.

In terms of human behaviour, anger equals aggression. Even cold, silent anger is tacit aggression. And the instinctive human response to aggression is fear and/or counter-aggression. So, demonstrating anger is more-or-less guaranteed to create a negative response on the part of the child, and to escalate the tension.

If you are not thinking clearly because of your emotional state, imagine how the equivalent emotion will affect a young person with underdeveloped pre-frontal lobes whose judgment, at the best of times, is more emotional than rational.

Understanding that in an angry state, nothing is to be gained by attempting to deal with any issue—especially one relating to behaviour which has touched a sensitive nerve—we must train ourselves to step back and allow logic to take over.

The head, not the heart, is the peacemaker.

There are steps we can take to engage the 'logic circuits', while disengaging the emotions—or at least their more disruptive influences.

a) We remove the immediate external source of the emotion—in this case, the 'offending' child—using the 'time-out'.

As mentioned earlier, there is a double advantage to this. Firstly, it allows us to regain emotional control and avoid saying something which we might find difficult to 'unsay' later.

Secondly, if we can manage to issue the instruction calmly, sending the child away (to his or her room, perhaps), with the instruction to 'think about what just happened', it forces the child to consider the effects of their actions on others. It also prepares them to be more receptive to constructive correction during the discussion or conciliation strategy which will follow.

b) We ask ourselves questions designed to force us into an examination of the real issues at stake in the situation.

These questions are specifically designed to focus our attention on:
i) The emotional source of our reaction—why the incident is important enough to affect our emotions.

Focusing on the underlying issues helps us to better understand the elements underpinning our perspective, and this aids us significantly in developing a compromise position.

ii) The likely motivation of the child at the time of the offence.

If we accept that most human beings who are not sociopaths have a reason for the majority of their actions, which is 'in tune' with their wider belief structure, then we are programming our non-conscious to seek out such reasons.

Questions like: 'Why am I so upset by this?' or 'Why is X so important to me?' force us to examine our own responses and help to disperse the anger. By focusing on the cause of the emotion, we move its centre away from the primitive and unthinking amygdala into the more sophisticated neural structures of the pre-frontal cortex, where evaluation, analysis and comparison take place.

This is not the domain of blind emotion, and once logic and introspection are applied to a reactive emotion like anger, its intensity is inevitably diminished.

Questions like: '*What makes Sam do this, when he knows the reaction he's likely to get?*' or '*Would Bianca really set out to hurt me like this, or could she have some other reason for acting in this way?*' force us to remember that this behaviour is 'extraordinary' and that perhaps the effect was unintended—thus setting up a 'search programme' which anticipates the child's perspective, opening us to the possibility of reconciliation and resolution.

c) We focus on the desired outcome of the situation, and the best way to achieve it.

It is important to examine the questions we can ask ourselves to put our 'anger-reaction' into some logical context. Understanding why we feel as we do, and attempting to understand what drove the 'offending' behaviour is a good start. However, a simple, practical approach to replacing anger with a more appropriate response can be trained during times when no anger is present, so that it becomes a default response under stress.

In any conflict situation, once we have considered the causes of the emotion (and the intent of the child), our behaviour should be based on *the desired outcome* and how that outcome might best be achieved.

When emotions are running high, however, it is difficult to consider the options rationally, so that the tendency might be 'to punish her', or 'to teach him a lesson he'll never forget'—creating a short-term 'resolution', by appeasing the emotion, but doing long-term damage to the parent/child relationship.

Using a time-out and the reframing questions will temper the emotion, but a future-focussed frame of mind can move us on to the next level—finding a resolution which teaches the child a better way of behaving and reduces the likelihood of a recurrence of the behaviour.

Try this approach on the opposite page.

HOW TO APPLY THE KNOWLEDGE

'Resetting the Default Response' by Focusing on Outcomes

Try this exercise to prepare you for the times when you may find it hard to think of the best response. The more we practice the process under low-stress conditions, the more easily we will be able to switch into the right mode of thinking during conflict situations.

We call it 'resetting the default response', and it can be done as a couple (the preferred method), or alone.

Step One:

Brainstorm ten recent times when you have been angry or upset with your children/students.

Step Two:

List the results from Step One, and write next to each one:

a) the desired/ideal outcome

b) your response

c) whether your response yielded the desired outcome

You could use a table like this one:

INCIDENT	DESIRED OUTCOME	RESPONSE	DESIRED RESULT (Y/N)
Abby lying about the broken plate.	Abby understanding the value of telling the truth and the consequences of her actions on others.	Got angry. Grounded Abby for a week. Stopped pocket money to pay for the plate.	No. Abby resentful and angry—no resolution or discussion of the incident. No learning.

Mrs Thorne complaining about Timmy stealing flowers from her garden.	Timmy learning the importance of respecting other people's property.	Half-hour time-out. Discussed the situation—got his reasons. Agreed on his punishment.	Yes. Timmy took the flowers as 'a present for Mum'. He now understands it was wrong—because Mrs Thorne works hard to grow them. Decided that Timmy should apologise and offer to help Mrs Thorne in the garden. She was pleased. When he finished helping, she gave him an ice-cream—and some flowers for Mum. Timmy learned a valuable lesson.
Timmy refusing to eat his peas (every time).	Timmy to understand that all kinds of food are good for him and should be eaten.	Forced him to sit there until he finished every pea.	No. Timmy got hysterical and started gagging on every mouthful. Eventually sent him to bed crying. He hates peas even more now.

Step Three:

For each example of a response that didn't work (a 'No' in column 4), brainstorm responses that are more likely to produce the desired outcome. Next time a similar situation occurs, try one out and see if it produces a better result.

Practicing the 'desired outcome' strategy in a low pressure environment, makes it easier to think on your feet when faced with the real thing.

2. How to Banish Blame

'Love me when I least deserve it, because that's when I really need it.'
Swedish Proverb

We have already quoted Robert Green Ingersoll in this book. Ingersoll rose from virtual poverty in 19th Century America to become one of the leading figures of his day. He was a man who counted among his friends (and, at times, his opponents) such leading lights as literary greats Mark Twain and Walt Whitman and Presidents Abraham Lincoln, Rutherford B. Hayes and James A. Garfield.

He was the greatest American orator of his day, and one of the greatest of all time. Despite the fact that he had almost no formal education before the age of twenty, he managed to become a highly successful lawyer whose clients included the great railway companies, at a time when the railways were at the height of their power. In middle and later life, he exerted great influence on the country's highest political office. When he died on the eve of the 20th Century, he was one of the richest men in America.

In many ways, Robert Ingersoll was a contradiction, but while the life and exploits of this great orator, lawyer, political activist and writer did not always live up to the highest ideals set down in his writings, his intuitive grasp of life's essential qualities and contradictions made him a famous, if flawed, champion.

Ingersoll, who was agnostic, believed in the power of the individual to take control of his/her own destiny—as he himself had done. Part of that process, he believed, was to understand the law of cause and effect, and to attempt to remove from the process all subjective judgments—emotional, social and even religious—which clouded the rationalist process.

In this vein, Ingersoll once wrote: *'In Nature, there are neither rewards nor punishments—there are consequences'*, [43] and though this observation was penned well over a century ago, it is just as important today as it was in the Victorian era—perhaps because, despite all our amazing advances, we are still operating on social and behavioural models which were set down at, or before, the end of the 19th Century.

The US Army has a process known as the 'After Action Review', during which all incidents and actions are analysed for the lessons which might be learned from them. This is not an exercise in blame-shifting, but merely a process whereby the facts of the situation might be brought out.

During this review individuals involved in an incident are asked three questions:

- What happened?
- What do you think caused it to happen?
- What can we learn from it?

The fact that a number of different participants are answering these questions gives a variety of perspectives and opinions from which the 'truth' can be synthesised—a process which takes advantage of the cognitive diversity of the group in question.

If the process is free from the threat of blame, much can be learned from this approach. Of course, in everyday life, it is not always easy to avoid the threat of blame. We live in a world which places great importance on assigning blame and issuing punishment. Often, however, blame and punishment are adjudged based on the results of an action, rather than its intent.

This is because, in legal and practical terms, it is far easier to examine results than it is to prove intent. In societies—and in individuals—however, the habit of assigning blame based on the outcome, rather than examining the incident using the wider lens of intent, demonstrates a worrying ethical immaturity—a logical blind-spot.

Such immaturity is acceptable—even expected—in the inexperienced young, but we need to train ourselves to be aware of the times when we ourselves are guilty of it.

Imagine this situation:

A man confronts a stranger in the street, intent on robbing him. The stranger has no money and the man becomes angry. He raises his gun, aims it at the victim's head and pulls the trigger.

Now, consider two scenarios. In the first, the bullet enters the victim's brain through the forehead, killing him instantly. In the second, the man's aim is slightly off, and the bullet glances off the victim's skull, wounding him, but doing no permanent damage.

In both scenarios, the shooter is apprehended and taken before the courts, but in each case, the charge—and the potential punishment—is different. Murder for the first, attempted murder for the second.

Measured on the scale of moral intent, is the crime of attempted murder any less a crime than that of murder? If the objective in each case was to take a life, then the crime in each case was the same, and just because one person was lucky—or incompetent—enough not to achieve the intended result, is that any reason to treat him more leniently than the person who in fact succeeded? Yet, look at the different sentences which we as a society mete out to someone convicted of murder, in comparison to the person convicted 'only' of attempted murder—especially in countries and states which have the death penalty.

As social creatures, we are influenced significantly by the attitudes and practices of the social environment surrounding us. Most of our criminal and civil legislation is designed primarily to protect person and property, and as such, it places great emphasis on the material results of an action—especially in deciding punishment and damages.

Some jurisdictions even allow for personal 'impact statements' from the victim or the victim's family-members. These statements are read into the record before sentencing—on the principle, it seems, that the gravity of the material consequences of any criminal act should be matched in relative terms by the severity of the punishment.

This means that, in terms of our sense of justice and our tendency to assign blame, as we are naturally guided by society's social and legal practices, we are likely to apply the same standards to crimes of a more everyday nature.

Think of the child (we'll call him Ricky) who, despite numerous warnings, still insists—through negligence or preoccupation—on leaving the front door open when he enters the house. The wind, passing down the passageway, slams the door closed every time, and every time, I shout at him to, *'Close the door next time—or else!'*

This time, however, when the door slams, my grandmother's irreplaceable heirloom plate, dislodged by the constant vibrations, crashes to the ground and smashes.

Do I still shout at him to *'Close the door next time—or else!'*?

Or do I blame him for the loss of the plate, and apply some more serious sanction?

Yes, the plate was smashed, and yes, the slamming door caused the accident, but what was the intention? The 'crime' on this occasion was no different from all the other times before it. Why, now, is the response so markedly different?

Obviously the significant material—or emotional—loss has elevated the child's action (or rather, his inaction) to a whole new level of seriousness, as evidenced by my punitive response.

But is this 'just'? From Ricky's perspective, am I not overreacting?

'I didn't mean it.' he thinks. 'It was an accident. It's not my fault.'

'I've warned you a thousand times about slamming that door!' I shout. Actually, it was seventeen, but the exaggeration isn't the key issue here. Let's examine the statement more carefully.

Did I warn him that the slamming door might have the effect of smashing Nanna's plate? Probably not. If I had foreseen the possibility, I would—or should—have taken precautions to prevent the eventuality. After all, if I did foresee it, and took no precautions, it would actually be my 'fault'—my negligence—wouldn't it? So, if I didn't predict it, how could I realistically expect Ricky to?

Therefore, the intention was not to smash the plate—making the incident an accidental consequence of an habitual behaviour.

So, do we punish people for accidents?

In wider society, we certainly do. Try accidentally running your car into another vehicle and see how quickly you are expected to pay for the damage. But this—again—is a practical matter of social economics. The damage must be repaired and someone has to pay, so the person 'at fault', whether the action was accidental or not, is deemed the one responsible for repairing the damage.

The key factor here, however, is that when we take our car out of the garage in the morning, we are aware of the rules of the game, and our decision to drive implies our tacit acceptance of those rules.

In the 'slamming door' situation, we have established very different rules. The rule is that when the door slams, a token threat is issued and no action takes place. A pattern of behaviour emerges based on this rule, and it is only when the unexpected—and accidental—breakage occurs that the rule suddenly changes.

This is inconsistent, confusing and, to the child, unfair behaviour. Any punishment meted out under these circumstances will, therefore, be resented.

Logically, Ricky is not to blame for the broken plate.

He is responsible for the door being left open, and even for the door slamming, if it is assumed that he should have predicted that consequence. But that is all. So, for me to punish him for smashing the plate is demonstrably 'unfair' and he is justified in feeling hard done by.

Then how do we deal with the situation? After all, the plate has been destroyed, and someone has to take the blame…

They *do*?

Why is it so important to find the person 'responsible' for every event that occurs? What is the purpose of blame?

> *Psychologically, assigning blame allows us to place responsibility for our sad, angry or negative feelings outside ourselves. It absolves us. It avoids any diminishing of our all-important 'standing' in the society, peer-group or family—or in our own mind. It is a symptom of a reactive mindset.*

Fact: The plate is gone.

Fact: No amount of finger-pointing and no punishment in the world is going to bring it back.

So why not use the situation as a growth opportunity instead? A healthier and more productive way to approach this kind of crisis situation is to apply a 'cause and effect' strategy.

During the short time-out to allow me to control my emotions and to allow the child to consider his role in the situation, I ask myself, *'Why am I so upset by this?'* or *'Why is the broken plate so important to me?'* This helps to focus my logic faculties on the underlying emotional reality.

It was the only memento I had of Nanna. / It was worth a thousand dollars—I could have sold it to help pay for a holiday. / It was the most beautiful object in the house, and I'm going to miss looking at it.

All of these possibilities—and a thousand others—create a feeling of disappointment and upset. Tie them to an act of disobedience or negligence, however, and the hurt transmutes to anger—and blame.

Emotionally, if I am feeling like this, then someone (Ricky) must be to blame. He deserves a punishment—'for his own good'—so that he won't behave like this again and make someone else (me) feel this way again.

But now the logic circuits, not the emotions, are operating, and if I have developed the habit of asking 'establishment questions', my next question looks at Ricky—his actions and his intent.

'Would Ricky really set out to hurt me like this, or could this just have been an unfortunate accident?'

This question is the beginning of a move from blame to a resolution of the situation, and signals that I am now ready to discuss the incident.

Of course, there are plenty of situations which are not accidents, where the child has deliberately acted in a way which has produced a negative outcome. Where he/she is, in fact, responsible for that outcome.

In these cases, as in the previous example, the ultimate goal is to bring the child to see the effect that his/her inappropriate action has produced—to undertake, where possible to fix or redress the resulting situation, and to avoid such behaviour in the future. If punishment or some sanction is a part of that learning process, then it should be presented as such to the child.

This doesn't mean the old, *'I'm going to teach you a lesson you'll never forget'* approach, while reaching for the strap. It means that the discussion focuses first on what happened—an examination of cause and effect.

'Tell me what happened,' is usually a good start.

The child knows that I probably know what happened, or we wouldn't be having the discussion, but the question gives him a chance to give his own perspective on the incident, and this is important—as it forces a level of self-analysis into the mix.

The discussion moves on to the resulting situation, and hopefully an examination of the reasons for the child's actions. In any 'blame-worthy' situation I can ask questions like these:

- Did you intend this to happen?
- Can you see how acting this way has affected your brother/ your friend/ the teacher?
- Do you think that Felicity really deserved it? Even if she does, can you think of any better ways you could have handled the situation?

We can all justify our actions in terms of what the other person did/deserved/ should have done. The trick is to get the child to admit that there is never just one response to any situation—that perhaps a different action would have produced a better outcome. For all parties. This is a necessary step in the growth of a young person towards responsible adulthood.

Often, what we are looking at within the behaviour which we wish to modify—the key 'failing'—is the child's inability to see beyond his/her own perspective. This is the 'me-occupation' of childhood and adolescence, which grows from the young person's inability to grasp, or rather to empathise with, a point of view which differs significantly from his/her own.

In the next section, 'How to Refine Responsibility', we will look in more detail at strategies for expanding the child's ability to recognise the effects of his/her actions on others—the idea of responsibility as the ability to make judgments and decisions balancing the needs of both 'self' and 'other'—but first we must look at one particularly destructive form of blame.

This is, of course, guilt—or self-blame.

Dealing With Self-Blame

'Rather than teaching our children to be 'self-reliant', or 'self-determined', or even 'self-motivated', we should first encourage them, in any way we can, to become 'self-caring'.' [44]

Miki Kanamaru

Children are often considered to be 'selfish', and while surface behaviour may appear to justify the charge, this judgment is perhaps a little harsh.

Selfishness implies both an awareness of the other person's needs, and a deliberate disregard of those needs. Selfishness, in other words, is a conscious decision. I have a choice, and I choose 'self' over 'other'.

Without effective training, children have little real choice when it comes to their motivations. They are simply inexperienced and developmentally ill-equipped to empathise or shift perspectives as most adults are capable of doing.

Rather than 'selfish', they might be more accurately characterised as 'self-centred' or 'self-oriented'.

While this often demonstrates itself in behaviour which takes little account of its effect on other people or their feelings, it can, in traumatic or highly emotional situations, lead to an equally unreasonable feeling of self-blame, such as 'survivor's remorse' or the unreasonable assumption of responsibility for events beyond anyone's control.

Left untreated, such traumatic self-blame can lead to serious psychological problems in later life, and should therefore be dealt with by an experienced professional. However self-blame which grows from the normal day-to-day mistakes and misbehaviour of the child can be dealt with using a few simple strategies.

Self-blame, or guilt, is a natural response, even in the young, when a misdeed and its effect on others is brought to the conscious attention. But though many parents like to use guilt as a method of behaviour-control, it should be remembered that self-blame, like any other form of blame, is backward-looking and counter-productive if not used to create a new learning; a new strategy for the future.

Some religions—and cultures—focus more strongly than others on encouraging guilt as an active 'policing mechanism', and this process occurs from a very young age. Unfortunately, though this may produce an apparently law-abiding and obedient citizen, the surface conformity often masks a nest of contradictions beneath the civilised façade.

The almost puritanical obsession with morality in Victorian England often reached ludicrous lengths. Classical artworks were reworked to protect the modesty of naked subjects, fashions covered all but facial flesh—even the legs of furniture were dressed.

The flavour of religious sermons was 'fire and brimstone'; hell and damnation awaited the slightest transgression of sinful Man. After all, didn't the Bible tell us that 'the wages of Sin is Death'? [45] Punishments were harsh and jails were full. But good, 'upstanding' gentlemen (and ladies) were everywhere. Weren't they?

Sadly, the veneer of moral rectitude masked a social reality—across the entire spectrum of society—which included disturbing levels of domestic violence, alcohol and opiate abuse, paedophilia and sexual perversion—and the highest per capita incidence of prostitution and venereal disease in British history. It even spawned the term 'Victorian morality' as a synonym for hypocrisy.

Apparently, guilt is not such an efficient policeman—for society, or for the individual. And certainly not for the impressionable, developing child.

The internalisation and institutionalisation of self-blame—especially in the home environment—is the last thing we need, if we are going to build a 'champion mindset' in our children. They will experience enough self-blame in their lives without our amplifying it.

A better approach is to use the exquisite focusing quality of guilt to create positive outcomes.

A situation is never quite so vividly in focus as when it is viewed through the lens of self-blame. This is why guilt-associated events can be so deeply felt and so terribly hard to dislodge from the psyche.

Of course, like any other subjective perspective, guilt is rarely, if ever, completely rational. It tends to feed on itself—to create associations with other aspects of experience, by priming the non-conscious with a negative search-programme.

What we need to do, is to break the negative cycle of self-blame, and use its impetus to create positive learnings.

How to Convert Self-Blame in Four Steps

'How unhappy is he who cannot forgive himself.' [46]

Publilius Syrus

Guilt is a universal human emotion—and therein lies its danger. Being an emotion, it often exists without a rational basis. Unless we develop a strategy for analysing the situation in a more objective way, then the only response left to us in the face of guilt is emotional.

Motivators and counsellors in all areas (including the brains behind at least one famous international weight-loss organisation) understand this. To combat the negative effects of guilt, many use a variation of this four-step approach. It is designed to convert self-blame into a more balanced 'self-caring' and the adoption of positive future behaviours.

Step One: Forgive Yourself

Unless the child has some unusually severe behaviour problems, each 'lapse' should be treated as an isolated event—an opportunity to learn and grow for the future.

If it is a 'relapse' (a failing similar to one which has occurred previously), it means that the potential learning was not taken from the previous situation—or was not internalised effectively enough to alter future behaviour. But the past is gone. It cannot be changed. The key, for the parent, is to avoid tying the current situation to the unresolved past one.

Guilt, like many other emotional responses, is a cumulative phenomenon. Dwelling on past mistakes connects the current guilt to whatever residual guilt still lingers from the previous incident. Psychologists term this process a *gestalt*. All we can realistically attempt to do is change future behaviour, so dwelling on past failures is ultimately unproductive.

Think, for a moment, of the toddler.

Some children take their first step and never look back, some stand and fall for days or weeks before learning to maintain balance. Some walk for a while, then return to crawling again, until they are motivated to walk sometime further down the track. We don't—or shouldn't—become frustrated and impatient with our child's efforts at walking. It is a natural process, and we know that it takes time—more for some children than for others.

We need to develop the same patience with behavioural development.

Lapse or relapse, the goal must be to analyse and understand the mechanism which led to the behaviour in the first instance, then put in place strategies which prevent it occurring again. This can only be achieved if the child is empowered to move beyond the incident and examine it in a more dispassionate way—and this is only possible if he/she has learned self-forgiveness.

At this point, you might be thinking that this approach provides the child with an 'easy out'. *Do the crime, avoid the time…* But nothing is further from the truth.

To forgive oneself is not the same as relinquishing responsibility for the action or its consequences. We are not talking here about denial—rather we are encouraging the child to confront the actual results of his/her actions, but in a way which promotes a deeper understanding of the effect of those actions on others.

The emotional guilt-response is unproductive, because as bad as the child might feel at an emotional level, the lack of rational analysis prevents any meaningful change for the future.

Like most of the strategies in this book, this step involves asking a couple of key questions.

i) Can you understand the reasons that things turned out the way they did?

ii) If you were in the same situation again—what would you change or do differently?

Both questions are asking the child to evaluate—consequences, in the first instance, choices in the second.

The emotion of guilt can easily overwhelm the analytical aspect of the child's mind and prevent learning from taking place. These two questions look at cause and effect, acknowledging the child's role in a less subjective way by focussing attention on the action at the heart of the negative emotion and looking forward to better future decisions.

Sometimes a child will find it easier to forgive him/herself if given the opportunity to do something to make up for the action in question. It is far better if this something is related in some way to the 'mistake' or 'crime' itself.

It should not be seen as a punishment, but rather as some kind of positive compensation. It is not always possible to make amends, but where it is, the action can be very therapeutic.

The question:

What do you think would be a suitable way to make amends to... (the person who has been effected by your actions)?

empowers the young person to take positive action designed to reduce the feeling of guilt.

If a young person is unable to come up with a suitable action, the adult should already have prepared a few possibilities, which can be introduced by saying something like, '*Maybe you could try A, or B, or C...What do you think?*' Giving children the final choice is an important part of the process, if they are going to 'own' the action and gain the full benefit.

In the novel *To Kill a Mockingbird* by Harper Lee (a book which should be compulsory reading for all parents and all young people), Jem Finch is a young boy, who, in a fit of anger, destroys a number of plants in a bad tempered old woman's garden.

His father Atticus (one of the truly great characters of international literature) arranges a 'punishment' which is actually a life-changing lesson for the boy. Jem must read to Mrs Dubose every afternoon until she falls asleep. Although he begins his task reluctantly, what the boy learns from this experience teaches him more about tolerance and maturity than anything else in his short life.

A sanction which is positive, instructive, and directly related to the misdeed in question, can be a significant growth experience for any child.

Steps Two to Four of this strategy focus on analysis of the incident, the planning of future strategies and rehearsal of the desired behaviour—to ingrain it as the preferred response for the future.

Step Two: Analyse the Incident

The first two questions in Step One focus the child on the results—the operation of cause and effect in relation to the incident. This is achieved in a non-judgmental way, and the combination of both questions turns the child's attention towards the future—to what might be done better next time.

The first question—the 'What is the reason?'—is an evaluation, an opinion. The second—the 'what if'—is a hypothetical, forcing the child to move beyond the immediate situation and imagine a better outcome.

At a non-conscious level, this approach prepares the child to acknowledge the role of his/her actions in producing the negative outcome, without the unproductive and potentially damaging exercise in 'blame-levelling'. This process is not about blame—it is about learning.

The next step is to analyse the underlying causes—the factors which led to the behaviour in the first place. It is important to discuss how things might have been done differently, but of equal importance is to isolate the elements in the situation which led to the mistake being made in the first place. This way, they might be recognised in the future—and avoided, or dealt with more effectively—before they push the situation out of control.

Being analytical, the questions in this step are designed to get at the facts of the situation. They are the 'what', 'how', 'who' and 'where' questions. They do not ask for opinion or conjecture, and no judgment is made. They are designed to seek out information which can be used to build understanding of why the situation developed as it did.

- Where were you?
- Who were you with?
- What was happening at the time?
- What was being said?
- What were you thinking about?

- What did you say to yourself, when...?
- How/what did you feel?
- What did you do?

These questions will vary slightly according to the situation, but the key is to recognise that this is an information-gathering exercise—not an inquisition. Developing the questioning structure together is the first step towards the time when the child will eventually be able to ask these questions of him/herself.

The ultimate aim is to replace self-blame with an analysis and future planning strategy. It is about patterning, so in the early stages when the parent is assisting the process, it is important to emphasise the form of the questions—particularly the use of 'How?' and 'What?' as opposed to 'Why' questions.

Step Three: Plan for the Future

Based on the previous structured questions and a better understanding of what happened this time around, the child is ready now to plan the future behaviours. The questions in Step Three are all future tense:

Next time, if a similar situation occurs, what will you:
- Say to yourself?
- Say to your friends?
- Tell yourself to feel?
- Do?

These are the proactive questions, inviting the non-conscious to seek out new and more effective responses. Again, to help the inexperienced child discover his/her ability to create better solutions, we can model for the child using the same construction we did in Step One: *'Maybe you could try A, or B, or C... What do you think?'*

The key is to get the child to 'own' the new strategies. Only then will they become the 'strategies of choice'.

Step Four: Rehearsal

Conscious repetition, reiteration and rehearsal of important strategies or insights may not always be possible, but as we have seen, the non-conscious mind is a powerful ally. Try creating mini-posters of key positive strategies. Attach them to walls, inside wardrobes or exercise books, onto the surface of the desk etc., so that they act subliminally on the non-conscious awareness.

The power of a simple message in constant view cannot be underestimated. In the 1920s, IBM, the huge office machine manufacturer, increased sales, productivity and morale significantly simply by putting into every office and workstation a small poster containing a single word.

That word was 'THINK'. This single word became the most quoted corporate slogan in history.

Talking about the strategies in 'round-table' discussions is also a way of reinforcing their effectiveness.

HOW TO APPLY THE KNOWLEDGE

Learning from the 'After Action Review'

Finding someone to blame is a national pastime. Listen to politicians, people at work or family members. We each want to avoid the consequences of being wrong—to find someone else to hold responsible for anything negative that happens—but as we have seen this is a non-productive, sometimes destructive approach.

From now on, each time you find yourself denying or assigning blame ('It's not my fault!' 'It's his/her/their fault!'), bite your tongue and try to adopt the approach of the US Army, and ask the more productive questions:

1. What happened?

2. What do you think caused it to happen?

and

3. What can we learn from it?

Remember, the goal—whether dealing with unacceptable behaviour, or the guilt and self-blame that it can engender—is to change future behaviour, not to dwell on the mistakes of the past.

The effective character-development strategy moves beyond the backward-looking assignment of blame and concentrates on the learning that can be gained to prevent a similar action and result in the future. Under this forward-looking approach, the child sees the effect of the action *on others* and accepts a sanction as part of the result of the wrong choice.

As we move beyond merely finding who is responsible for what happened, perhaps we also need to change our notion of exactly what responsibility is.

3. How to Refine Responsibility

'I'm a very responsible person. Every time anything bad happens, they tell me I'm responsible.'

Anonymous Teenager

This section is called 'How to Refine Responsibility', but perhaps the real secret lies first in learning how to define responsibility.

The phrase, *'He's responsible for that,'* is usually just another way of saying, *'He's to blame,'* and this is another example of how language often evolves away from its original meaning.

In its original form, the word 'responsible' implied being trustworthy, capable of rational conduct and accountable (as in: 'responsible government', 'a responsible person', 'a grave responsibility'). With the growth of the universal bureaucracy during the 19th and 20th Centuries and the shift in the concept of accountability to the notion that 'someone must be ultimately responsible' whenever anything goes wrong, came the habit of equating the word 'responsibility' with blame.

One consequence of this is the sort of attitude that we glimpse in the words of the anonymous teenager in the opening quote of this section. When the words 'responsible' or 'responsibility' carry such negative connotations, how can we ever expect our children to willingly accede to our demand that they 'show more responsibility' or 'try to be more responsible'.

One great advantage of banishing blame from the home or school environment is that it makes it easier to promote the concept of developing responsibility.

In Part One, we introduced the notion of a young person's 'right to responsibility' and suggested that we gradually introduce responsibility to young people; that 'to learn responsibility, they need to practice being responsible.'

So, how do we do this? How do we refine responsibility in our children?

The simple answer is that we create an expectation of responsible behaviour on the part of the child by requiring the same expectation of ourselves—by demonstrating responsible behaviour through our own actions and reactions.

This cannot be achieved without a high level of active communication between adult and child. We must talk about and negotiate responsibilities in all areas of life—from household chores, to caring for pets, from public and social behaviour to relationships within the family.

We must provide responsible behaviour models and set negotiated 'ground rules'— models and structures against which responsible behaviour can be measured.

And, above all, we must teach them to ask the right questions.

Having rejected blame as our primary response mechanism, we first replace it with an approach which emphasises the analysis of cause and effect.

Recalling Robert G. Ingersoll's observation quoted earlier, we concentrate our energies on evaluating the consequences of past actions and the predicting of consequences of future actions.

Responsible behaviour is behaviour that learns lessons, both from previous successes and previous failures, then uses those lessons to evaluate the response options available under current circumstances, to predict results and identify the preferred options.

If the lessons of responsibility are well-learned, the 'preferred option' will be the one which takes into account the consequences of the resulting action on both 'self' and 'other'.

The Ethical Spectrum

'Live so that when your children think of fairness and integrity, they think of you.' [47]

H. Jackson Brown

The following diagram represents the continuum between 'self' and 'other', and serves as a simple and practical model for analysing both responsibility (in the wider sense of the word) and consequences, in relation to an individual's actions.

The 'Ethical Spectrum'

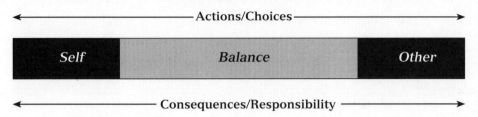

In children and pre-adolescents, the 'Me-orientation' is strong—the world is an extension of 'Me' and my actions and responses are grounded in that perspective. For this reason, the behaviour of most children, unless it is moderated by adult intervention, falls very clearly into the left-hand area of 'Self'. Actions and choices are based on their effect on 'Me' and my perceived needs and consequences are evaluated using the same criteria.

A young child is essentially blind to the effects of his/her behaviour on others—except when that behaviour produces an action in response which impacts back on the young child him/herself.

Teenagers on the other hand, are often hostage to their hormones, and frequently, especially in times of crisis or emotional overload, lose the ability to move beyond the cycle of their own immediate and sometimes ill-judged motivations.

We are social animals, however, and as we grow, our 'Me-orientation' gradually evolves through our numerous social interactions—a sort of mathematical averaging-out of the various 'Me-oriented vectors' surrounding us. As a result, by adulthood, most of our choices and actions fall into the area of 'Balance' between the 'Self' and the 'Other'.

The important question is: How much of our social behaviour is actually determined by fear of the social consequences of selfish behaviour, and how much by an innate 'responsibility'?

How 'balanced' would our choices be if there were no social sanction against a selfish behaviour—if, say, there were no one watching, or virtually no chance of 'getting caught'?

Consider this situation:

> *You are waiting to use an automatic teller machine. The man in front of you is old, and obviously unused to the 'new-fangled' technology. He is showing his frustration with the machine, believing it to be faulty, and*

when his card is returned to him, he grabs it and storms off, not realising that by taking the card he has released the money.

As you step up to take your turn, before you can insert your card, the machine presents you with a wad containing three hundred dollars. There is no one in the line behind you, and the old man is twenty metres away, still mumbling frustratedly to himself.

What would you do, and, by consequence, what would you hope your child might do?

(a) Pocket the money and think yourself lucky.

(b) Run after him and give him back the money, but respond to his offer of a twenty-dollar reward by telling him that considering you could have taken it all, perhaps fifty dollars is more appropriate.

(c) Run after him and give him back the money, accepting his offer of a twenty-dollar reward gratefully.

(d) Run after him and give him back the money, refusing to accept any reward.

(e) Run after him and give him back the money, refusing to accept any reward, but offering instead to show him how to use the machine properly, so that he will have no problem next time.

It is relatively easy to place these five choices in their appropriate positions on the 'Ethical' continuum. (a) is firmly in the 'Self'; (b) would just make it into the 'Balance'; (c) is quite well-balanced and (d) is entering the 'Other'—but what about (e)? By offering to go out of your way to help another person, with no purpose other than to improve his life, you have established the response securely in the 'Other' zone of the continuum.

And what if your response was to run after him and give him back the money, accepting his offer of a twenty-dollar reward with the intention of donating it to the latest Earthquake Appeal? Again, an 'Other' choice—this time, one through which you transform your good fortune (and the old man's) into a positive outcome for a wider group of 'others'.

How do we measure responsibility? Ultimately, it is by acknowledging (and predicting) the effect of our decisions and actions on others. By considering what, historically, idealists have always called 'the greater good'.

This is what underpins the teachings of all the great religions and social philosophies of the world. It is what separates the truly 'great' individual from the merely 'successful' one.

Social responsibility is not calculated by the emotional responses of the amygdala or the survival drives of the limbic system; it is not even a merely logical response to any analysis of cause and effect. It is a mindset which grows out of a particular behavioural patterning.

> *Social responsibility is a learned behaviour; a decision-making strategy based on a mental process which can be learned—and habituated—so that it becomes an important part of the way we analyse cause and effect. It has the power to affect all our decision-making. And, like any other habit, responsibility is most effectively trained in childhood.*

If you are philosophically-minded, you might be thinking at this point that our definition of responsibility is sounding a lot like a definition of morality—and in a sense you would be right.

'Morality', according to most dictionaries, is the science of determining right and wrong—that is, of attempting to achieve the good outcome over the bad one.

A 'moral' decision balances the wants and needs of the individual against the wants and needs of any others affected by that decision.

The 'immoral' decision, on the other hand, takes into account only self, while the 'amoral' decision is concerned with a specific—usually practical—goal and does not consider the consequences for individuals at all.

Hence, the socially responsible decision is also (except under the most blindly fundamentalist definition of morality) a moral decision.

For each of us, ultimately, how we behave must be dictated by a grasp of the effect that behaviour will have on others—and not by a set of arbitrary rules enforced by anyone with the power to impose compliance.

We can make our children 'do the right thing' (translation: 'do what they are told'), or we can guide them to the understanding of what is fair and right for everyone affected in any decision they may make during their lives.

The first way trains an obedient, compliant and unquestioning 'fundamentalist' mentality. The second encourages mature ethical behaviour which is responsive to whatever situation may be confronted into the future. (For a more sophisticated dual-axis model of the 'Ethical Spectrum', see Case Study 3.)

Employing a raft of computer-age technologies, the work of thousands of researchers worldwide has revealed not only the areas of the brain utilised during particular mental activities—the 'cartography' of the living brain—but also the fact that the focus on and repetition of certain conscious and volitional thought habits can have the effect of permanently altering patterns of thinking and even actual brain structures.

For a detailed account of one man's life-work in this area, read *The Mind & the Brain—Neuroplasticity and the Power of Mental Force* (2002) by Jeffrey M. Schwartz and Sharon Begley.

Jeffrey Schwartz is a psychiatrist who discovered during his work with patients suffering Obsessive Compulsive Disorder (OCD) that by focusing their attention away from negative behaviours and toward positive ones, his patients were able to make permanent changes to their own neural pathways, proving that, '*we have the power to [consciously] shape our brains, and, consequently, our destiny.*' [48]

It has long been known that during certain periods of development, the human brain undergoes phases of significant growth and pruning, but this was originally thought to be purely a genetically controlled and automatic process.

The work of researchers like Schwartz, quantum physicist Henry Stapp and numerous others worldwide shows that structural change in the brain is possible throughout a person's life, and that we can learn to have a certain amount of conscious control over the direction of that change.

In the next Volume: *The Art of Learning How to Learn,* we will explore in more detail the implications of this discovery for the development of advanced active learning strategies.

The exciting thing about tying our new understandings of the learning brain to the notion of responsibility (and morality) is that we now have a realistic model for teaching our children how to distinguish right from wrong, good from bad—better from best.

This learning has a logical—even a neurological—basis. In this model, social responsibility—morality—is more than simply a list of rules to be memorised and examined for inspiration and guidance.

It is not rigid or fundamentalist, but fluid and responsive. It is a *way of thinking* that can be 'hard-wired' into the developing brain and strengthened through rehearsal and experience, until it is the preferred pathway for dealing with any important decision.

HOW TO APPLY THE KNOWLEDGE

Getting on with the Job

Responsibility is a learned behaviour, and the only way to learn it is to experience it—at an appropriate time and an appropriate level.

A simple way of building responsibility in children is to introduce it gradually, by making them responsible for aspects of family life, according to their abilities.

Even a young child can be made responsible for choosing his/her clothes ready for the morning. By allowing freedom of choice, praising good choices and helping the child to 'amend' inappropriate choices, we help the child to recognise the difference.

Being responsible for washing the dishes after meals, or keeping the room tidy, or other jobs like mowing the lawns or washing the car (for older children) can help instil a sense of pride, especially if accompanied by recognition of a job well done and other kinds of descriptive feedback.

Rights and privileges can be tied to the performance of responsibilities—to emphasise the consequences of behaviour, both responsible and irresponsible. Perhaps a points system can be instituted—a point for each time the child fulfils his/her responsibility (and extra bonus points for voluntary responsible behaviour which goes beyond what was expected of them), with an agreed number of points required before the child receives pocket money, or next week's allocated PlayStation time.

This is different from a bribe where a reward is offered if the child does something specific. Bribes are *ad hoc* and unpredictable, and do not create the habitual behaviour we desire, because the action is reward-oriented and specific to the one situation.

Linking ongoing privileges to ongoing responsibilities provides structure and consistency—and changes behaviour long-term.

4. How to Seek Solutions

'Too often we give children answers to remember, rather than problems to solve.' [49]

Roger Lewin

Robert Frost wrote about 'the road not taken' (having himself—in becoming a poet—chosen the one 'less travelled by'), and with that image, he reminded us that every decision is a turning point—a fork in the road. The choice of one solution over another.

Life is about choices, and preparing our children for a life of creative decision-making is one of the most important things that we, as parents and teachers, can do. Ultimately, what we teach them is to create their own story—the narrative of their own lives—through a series of choices.

In Part One, we looked at the proactive question and the brainstorm as a strategy of resolving conflicts. And what is conflict-resolution, except the choice of the best solution to a specific, usually emotional, problem?

If every choice is a fork in the road, then forming solutions, making decisions—writing our own story—is far too important to be left to chance. Or to the whims of our emotional selves.

Decision-making—the selection of a solution to any question or issue—must be a combination of structure and imagination. It must be a creative act.

Remember the proactive questions?

- 'How is it possible to achieve... (the desired result)?'
- 'What are the possible consequences, if... (the desired result) happens?'
- 'What are the possible consequences, if... (the undesired result) happens?'
- 'In the event of... (the undesired result) happening, what are the negative elements preventing... (the desired result) from happening, and how can these obstacles be overcome?'

In seeking solutions—no matter what area of life or activity we find ourselves considering—the use of the proactive question and the brainstorm which it promotes is a technique which can be trained, so that, over a period of time, it develops into a learning habit.

Once it becomes a habit, this process of thinking enters the realm of 'expertise', meaning that it operates as a semi-automatic routine—employed whenever decisions must be made.

Relating this process to everyday problem-solving and the power of the 'narrative intelligence' ties in closely to the work of Jerome S. Bruner.

Bruner—one of the 'greats' of 20th Century cognitive and educational psychology—ties learning, in its widest sense, and the creation of meaning in life, very closely to our grasp of narrative. For a brief discussion of his theory of the narrative process in our construction of reality, see Case Study 2.

In real life, however, it is not realistic to expect people to whip out a sheet of paper and scribble down a brainstorm or a table of priorities under any and all circumstances, and this is the real advantage of turning the thought process into a habit.

Think of any physical training regime—like training the jump shot in basketball. In the heat of the game, we want the player to be able to catch the ball, jump and release the shot over the defence in one fluid motion, but this can only happen if each of the elements *and their combination* has been trained into the 'muscle-memory'.

Training the 'muscle-memory' of intellectual processes—even creativity—can be achieved using a similar approach.

Of course, the key to success in sports is to understand that during the game is not the time to try to instill the correct technique. With the mind occupied by the ebb and flow of the action, and the emotions over-stimulated, there is no room left for thinking about technique.

In such a situation we are in 'reaction' mode, and our skills will only be effective if *we do not have to think about them*. They must be automatic routines—like driving a car, or brushing our teeth—routines which we can run while we are attending to other important things.

If there are three seconds left on the shot-clock and I am facing a defender who is taller and stronger than I am, I want my mind free to plan my move—fake left, drive right, pull up outside the three-point line, and 'launch a bomb' (take the three-point shot). The mechanics of the fake, the drive, the pull-up and the shot cannot be considered in detail—at least, not if I want to 'drain the three'.

When it comes to seeking out solutions to problems, the most important habit we can inculcate in young people is to step away from the emotion (feel it, accept it, understand it, but don't allow it to dictate your response); to isolate the key elements in the problem and understand how they are related. That is, to 'home in' on the chain of cause and effect, in order to see what can be changed to achieve/prevent a particular end result.

And these are skills best mastered in zero-pressure—preferably fun—environments, so that they become the favoured way of processing.

By focusing on modes of thinking and applying them over a wide range of experiences, we strengthen networks of neurons in key brain-sites and across the *corpus callosum* and develop habits of thinking that are 'transferable' between different situations.

> *Modern brain/learning theory (the work of researchers such as Jeff Hawkins, Stephen Grossberg, Gerald Edelman and Vernon Mountcastle for example) sees the learning brain as a pattern-recognition machine which simultaneously processes information, compares it with an existing template, makes and tests predictions, then uses the results to alter the pre-existing template. This means that the right training can pattern the existing template, and this positively influences the response to any future stimulus.*

An understanding of the notion of cause and effect is crucial to this process.

If a given combination of elements always produces a similar result, and that result is undesirable, then in order to avoid the undesirable result, we must prevent that combination of elements from happening. If, on the other hand, it is a desirable outcome, then we need to do what we can to ensure that that combination of elements occurs.

If a golfer swings the club the same way every time, and every time he hooks the ball left, then if he wants to hit the ball straight down the fairway, he must change his swing. You can't swing the same way and hit the ball differently. This is why a good golf-pro who can 'doctor' a poor swing is never out of work.

Broken down simply, any problem is solvable (and every goal achievable) to some extent simply by doing something (or a number of things) differently.

A problem is, by definition, a result we do not desire, and a solution is one that we do desire, so we would do well to remember Einstein's advice that: '*There can be no more certain sign of insanity than to do the same thing over and over, and expect the result to be different.'*

Creative problem-solving, lateral thinking, imagination and the association of previously unconnected ideas—what are often called right-brain activities, because much of their processing takes place in the right hemisphere—are also activities which draw on the particular talents of the frontal cortex.

We have already seen that the frontal cortex is the last area of the brain to mature, and nothing we can do can dramatically change the pace of that physiological development. There is evidence to suggest, however, that mental activities which promote connectivity within the frontal lobes form an excellent framework upon which to build creative thinking strategies as the individual matures.

> *I may desire the power of the six-litre V8, but if what I have right now is a two-litre four-cylinder, I can still do things to radically improve its performance until the more powerful vehicle is available. The same principle applies to the developing frontal lobes.*

With this in mind, one very valuable way for parents to prepare their children to be creative problem-solvers and solution-seekers is to establish within the daily or weekly routine a range of fun activities, many of which can be enjoyed as a family.

These activities promote neural patterning within the frontal lobes and build stronger links between the structured logic of the left hemisphere and the 'associative intelligence' of the right—building the child's intellectual 'muscle memory'.

These activities often take the form of lateral thinking or logical problem-solving games, which can range from the most elementary to brain-busters.

It is not within the scope of this book to provide a complete programme of these games and activities. Instead, in the 'How to Apply the Knowledge' section at the end of Part Three, we give examples of activity types and provide suggestions for inexpensive ways to access any number of similar activities.

In the process, we will also suggest ways to introduce the use of these puzzles and games into the family routine in a fun way, which not only promotes better thinking strategies for all members of the family, but also, if pursued enthusiastically, builds rapport and communication between family members and raises self-esteem.

Any reasonable bookshop will have at least one shelf dedicated to books of puzzles of various kinds. The most beneficial are lateral thinking puzzles, and puzzles which require the application of logic.

Games and puzzles which involve lateral thinking and/or logical problem-solving are a great training ground for the creative thinker.

Another readily available and virtually inexhaustible source of mind puzzles is, of course, the Internet. Typing the search 'logic and lateral thinking puzzles for children' into your favourite search-engine should keep you (and your family) busy—but beware. It is easy to get sucked into the puzzle pages and expend a significant amount of time before coming up for air.

Another good search is 'Mensa'—which will locate sites that, as well as offering tests which 'measure' your IQ to see if you are 'Mensa material', also have some fun puzzling activities.

We hear a great deal of talk about the need for 'quality time' between parents and their children of all ages, but rarely, if ever, is the talk accompanied by any definition of what makes it quality time. Certainly, it must be time which builds strong loving relationships; it should be relaxing and fun and add to the quality of life.

Spend time:
- playing puzzle games
- sharing interesting facts or observations
- indulging in joke-telling competitions
- reading, reciting or creating stories or poetry together
- listening to each other's music non-judgmentally, and explaining what excites/moves you about your favourite pieces
- discussing topical sports, politics, social or world events
- playing trivia, card or board games (especially those which require logic and/or spatial skills and/or strategy)

These and a hundred other activities are all quality ways of spending time, which promote healthy family relationships and strong thinking-skills in all members of the family—the parents included. And none of them involves a television or a computer.

HOW TO APPLY THE KNOWLEDGE

'Backwards understood be only can but, forwards lived be must life.' [(50)]

—Søren Kierkegaard

Here are some typical examples of different types of Lateral Thinking/ Logic Puzzles.

i) The Lateral Problem-Solving Exercises

Puzzle A.

A man has a goat, a fox and a bag of carrots which he has to get safely across a river, but his boat is only big enough to carry him and any one of these three across safely. Now he has a problem. He cannot leave the goat unattended with the carrots, or the goat will eat them. Also, he cannot leave the fox with the goat, or the fox will kill the goat. How does he get all three safely across to the other side?

Puzzle B.

Two mothers and two daughters enter a dress shop to look for outfits for a wedding which they are all attending. Each woman spends exactly $300, and the shopkeeper receives $900. No theft or discounts are involved, and the shopkeeper sees nothing wrong with the transaction. Where did the rest of the money go?

Puzzle C.

You have five pieces of chain of differing lengths, which you must link together into one length.

A

B

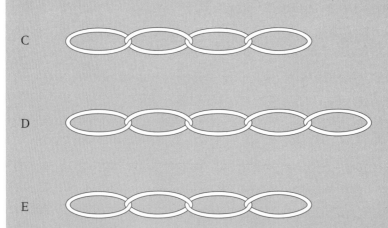

C

D

E

You could do it by opening the end link of length A (one move) and joining it to the beginning of length B (two moves), then opening the end link of length B (three moves) and joining it to the beginning of length C (four moves) etc. all the way to length E. That would take you eight moves. Can you do it in less?

ii) Logical Problem-Solving

Three friends arrive at the dance, each wearing a different colour. By a strange coincidence the three girls' names, Scarlet, Rose, and Amber, are the same as the three colours which they have chosen, though the names do not necessarily match with the colours they wear.

Here are four statements about the three girls. Unfortunately, only one statement is true:

• Scarlet is not wearing amber.

• Rose is not wearing scarlet.

• Scarlet is wearing scarlet.

• Rose is not wearing amber.

Which girl is wearing which colour?

iii) Plotting the Meaning of Language

Many logic puzzles demand a more sophisticated control of both the nuances of language and of spatial relationships, as in the following example:

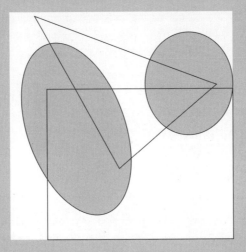

i) Write 1 in the rectangle so that it is not contained in any of the other figures.

ii) If it is false to deny that bananas are yellow, place 2 where it will be only in the triangle and the oval; otherwise put it in the triangle alone.

iii) If it is correct to deny that dogs are mammals, place a 3 under the 1, otherwise place 4 within the triangle, rectangle and circle.

iv) If 4 x 3 is closer to 10 than 7 x 2, put a 5 where rectangle and oval overlap; otherwise put it in the oval only.

v) If all rectangles are squares, place 6 where it will be within the rectangle and the triangle; otherwise put 7 there.

vi) We know that all even numbers are divisible by two. If it is illogical to deny that a number which is not divisible by two cannot be an even number, place 8 in the circle alone; otherwise cross out the 1 and write 9 there.

iv) In Other Words...

With the advent of SMS, text messaging and Internet chat-rooms, many young people have become adept at another form of lateral thinking, which involves creating and making sense—in a semantic context—of sound and picture clues to derive meaning. This is verbal shorthand translated into symbolic form, for the convenience of typing with a thumb on a mobile-phone keypad, or talking simultaneously in text to as many as ten (or more) different 'chat-room' contacts.

[It is interesting that this type of 'multi-tasking' does not seem to have the effect of 'swamping' their processing capabilities, in the way most other distractions seem to do. Perhaps there is food for a research programme or two there!]

We see the same facility in the imaginative ways that some young people 'personalise' their car registration plates:

DOMN8R– FOR 'DOMINATOR'

XLR8IN—FOR 'ACCELERATING'

LMN8R—FOR 'ELIMINATOR'

0INGIN—FOR 'ZEROING IN'

1-TED— FOR 'WANTED'

URDSYR—FOR 'YOUR DESIRE'

2BIZAR—FOR 'TOO BIZARRE'

EZ2C—FOR 'EASY TO SEE'

Lateral-thinking word puzzles use the arrangement, appearance, positioning and sound of individual letters or entire words to force the 'player' to make connections in a lateral way, by combining 'literal' meanings with other knowledge areas (often common sayings) to complete the puzzle.

Once children are hooked on these puzzles, it can be fun for them to create their own. Here are some simple examples:

WORD PUZZLES

1

THE ⊓ SKY

$\sqrt{}$ LUST
ENVY
PRIDE
SLOTH
ANGER
GLUTTONY
COVETOUSNESS

WORL
AMEN

PAID
I'M
WORKED

THE WEATHER
FEELING

EVER
EVER   **& EVER**
EVER
EVER

<table>
<tr><td>7</td><td>

READING

</td></tr>
</table>

8

<u>NE1410S?</u>

9

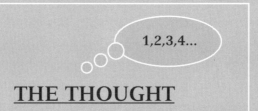

<u>THE THOUGHT</u>

10

THREFEACDE

v) Using Symbolic Logic

Type A.

Eloise is the youngest of five children. Her eldest sister is Amy, then come Bruce, Catherine and Daniel. When her grandfather died, he left $1,000 to be shared between his five grandchildren, but not equally. The money was divided according to the age of the children, so that each child received $50 more than the next youngest.

How much money did Eloise receive?

How much did each of her siblings receive?

Type B.

Many Logic Puzzles rely heavily on the ability to manipulate numbers—which is to be expected, as numbers are the most logical of all human creations. Many children (and adults) enjoy Sudoku and magic number squares, and there are many websites that offer access to these puzzles.

Apart from these and other specialised forms of number puzzle, many puzzles involving numbers also require the player to think laterally in order to work out how to manipulate the numbers.

Try these:

(a) The tree at the back of my house measures 15 metres plus a quarter of its own height. How high is it?

(b) A Planter and plant cost $41. If the planter costs $40 more than the plant, what does each item cost?

and the tough one:

(c) You have 12 'gold' coins, but only 11 are real. One of these coins is slightly heavier or lighter than the others. You have a two-dish balance scale. You are allowed to weigh only three times. Is it possible to identify the false coin?

SOLUTIONS

i) Lateral Thinking Puzzles

Puzzle A:

The trick to this problem is to realise that the man can carry things in both directions—this is why it is a lateral thinking problem. It cannot be solved simply by taking one 'passenger' over at a time, so the solution must employ at least one other element. The man must always have 'safe' combinations on either riverbank, and the only combination that is 'safe' to leave is the fox and the carrots, so how can he arrange it so that only this combination is ever left together?

1. First, he takes across the goat, leaving the fox and the carrots.

2. Next, he goes back and brings the fox, but this time when he returns, he takes the goat back. Now the fox is alone, and the man is in control of the goat, so the carrots are safe.

3. He leaves the goat on the original side of the river, and takes over the carrots.

4. He returns once more for the goat.

Puzzle B:

There is no other money, because only three women entered the store—a grandmother, her daughter and her granddaughter. In this way, there are in fact, two mothers and two daughters—one being both mother and daughter.

This solution involves lateral thinking, because we need to reconcile two apparently irreconcilable pieces of information (ie. Four people spent $300 each, yet the shop received only $900). If each woman spent $300, then there could only have been three women; if there were four women, then each could have only spent $225. As in most puzzles, close attention to the wording reveals that each woman did, in fact, spend $300, so the clue is in the opening statement: Two mothers and two daughters. The fact that this is so specific leads us to ask the question: How can two mothers and two daughters add up to three people? The answer: If one is both mother and daughter—if they are three generations of the one family. Which is the solution.

This could have been worked out using the Ideagram, based on the generator question: How can two mothers and two daughters add up to three people?

Puzzle C:

Of course you can. If you undo the three links of length A and use them to join the other lengths, you can do it in six moves. Try it.

Again, this is a lateral thinking puzzle, because it requires the player to abandon an obvious (and supplied) solution and look for another approach. Dismantling an entire length to use the parts individually is counter-intuitive, but it turns out to be 25 per cent more efficient. Imagine finding solutions like that for everything in your life.

ii) Logical Problem-Solving

The key to solving this kind of problem is to make sure we take notice of all the information we are given—not just the four statements.

1. Either the first or the fourth statement must be true, because they both can't be false. If both were false, then both girls would wear amber (and we know that there are three different colours).

2. Therefore either Scarlet or Rose is wearing amber.

3. As one of these statements is true (and as there is only one true statement), the second and third statements must be false.

4. The falsity of the second statement means that Rose is wearing scarlet and this also establishes that statement four is true, which means that statement one is false—which means that Scarlet is wearing amber.

5. Amber, therefore, must be wearing rose.

iii) Plotting the Meaning of Language

This type of puzzle is demanding, because it requires the overlap of a number of key skills—but this is also what makes it so valuable.

First, the language skills:

Each instruction requires the reader to deal with the complex relationships between two or more elements, using such elements as:

- The meaning-reversing effect of a sequence of negative terms (as in, If it is illogical [-ve] to deny [-ve] that a number which is not [-ve] divisible by two cannot [-ve] be an even number...)

- Following complex instructions, containing a number of multi-element alternatives (as in, If it is correct to deny that dogs are mammals, place a 3 under the 1, otherwise place 4 within the triangle, rectangle and circle.)

Second, the spatial skills:

Once the correct meaning of the instruction has been worked out, the task is not complete. The player is then required to use a different part of the brain to distinguish, visually, the spatial relationships within the geometric jigsaw puzzle on which the answers must be plotted.

- Where in the jumble of lines do the shapes overlap with no others?
- Where do the shapes overlap with only one other?
- Where do they overlap with two?
- Do any overlap with all three of the others?

Below is the solution.

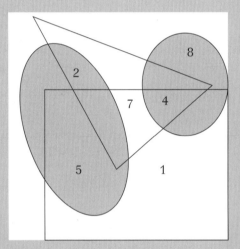

iv) In Other Words...

These are lateral thinking puzzles, because they force us to think about the words (and even the letters) in new ways—in terms of sound and position, etc. Here are the solutions:

1. Pie [pi] in the sky.

2. The root of all evil [square root sign and the seven deadly sins].

3. World without end [no 'd'], Amen.

4. I'm overworked and underpaid [a play on the relative positions of the words].

5. Feeling 'under the weather' [ditto].

6. For [four] ever and ever.

7. Reading between [literally] the lines.

8. Anyone [NE1] for [4] tennis [10S]?

9. It's the thought [note the thought bubble] that counts [1, 2, 3, 4...].

10. Red in [physically] the face.

These fun puzzles are a good start for sharing this type of activity. Encourage the children to bring new ones to the dinner table each night for a week or so—either ones they have found, or ones they have created—make it a team-sport.

v) Using Symbolic Language: Type A

This problem deals with numbers and patterns (each share increasing by a given amount according to a predetermined sequence). Such problems are best solved using symbols to represent the key elements. Once we see the relationship between each of the shares and the total amount left in the will, it is easy to work out the individual shares. In the end, what we have here is a simple piece of algebra.

i) We need to find how much Eloise gets, so we use a symbol (say 'X') to represent this number. This is the only unknown factor—everything else we have been told, so we set out the information in symbolic form.

- Eloise's share = X

- Daniel's share = X + 50

- Catherine's share = X + 100

- Bruce's share = X + 150

- Amy's share = X + 200

If all these shares add up to $1,000, then all we have to do is bring all the shares together, to calculate the value of X.

So:

$5X + \$500 = \$1,000$

$5X = \$500$

$X = \$100$

- Eloise receives $100
- Daniel receives $150
- Catherine receives $200
- Bruce receives $250
- Amy receives $300

Type B.

(a) Logically, if the tree has a quarter of its height above the 15 metres mark, then 15 metres must equal $^3/_4$ of its height. Therefore $^1/_4$ is 5 metres and the height is 20 metres.

Of course, if that didn't strike you right away, you can solve it this way using simple mathematics:

Call the height of the tree (H)

$$H = 15 + {}^H\!/_4$$

$$H - {}^H\!/_4 = 15$$

$$3\,{}^H\!/_4 = 15$$

$${}^H\!/_4 = 5$$

Therefore: $H = 5 \times 4 = 20$ metres

(b) Many people—illogically—give the answer as $40 & $1, not noticing that this makes the difference only $39. It 'feels' right, so they don't question it.

If the planter is $40 more expensive, all we have to do is to deduct the $40 from the total price, then split what is left equally between the two articles. Half of $1 is 50c. Which means that the Planter costs $40.50c and the plant 50c. Not a bad deal!

(c) This one is a real logic tester*. With only three weighings available, one solution (the only one we could work out, maybe you can work out another one) is this:

(i) Divide the coins into 3 piles of 4 coins each—call them A, B & C.

(ii) Place piles A & B on opposite sides of the scale.

If: (a) They are balanced, then the fake is not in either A or B, so it is one of the four coins in C. (b) They are unbalanced; the fake is one of the eight coins in the A or B piles. (Be careful to note which pile rises and which goes down, as this will be important later.)

(iii) For the second weighing, you have two options:

If: (a) The fake is not in either A or B, place two coins from A on one side of the scale (as the control), and two from C on the other side. If the two are balanced, the fake is one of the other two C coins. If not, the fake is one of the two C coins on the scale.

(b) If the fake is in A or B, place two A coins and two B coins on one side of the scale. Be careful to keep track of which are A's and which are B's. Place one B coin on the opposite side, and add three C coins (as the control). Isolate the A and B coins which you removed.

If the scale remains in balance, then the fake is one of the three coins not on the scale. If it is unbalanced, then it is important to note which direction the tilt is.

If the side with the single B coin sits in an opposite position (up or down) to the one which the B pile occupied in step (i), then the fake is not the single coin, but one of the two B coins on the other side. (If the fake was one of the A coins, they would not now be sitting opposite to their position in step (i)).

If the side with the single B coin sits in the same position (up or down) as the one which the B side occupied in step (i), then either the single B coin is the fake, or one of the two A coins—and again we have narrowed the possibles to three.

(iv) For the final weighing, you have one of three possibilities:

(a) If one of the two C coins is the fake—as in either of the (iii) (a) scenarios, simply weigh one of them against any of the A or B coins. If the scale remains in balance, then the other C coin is the fake—if not, then the C coin on the scale is the fake and YOU HAVE SOLVED THE PROBLEM.

(b) If the fake is one of the two B coins from the last weighing, follow the same process as in (a); weigh one of them against any of the A or C coins. If the scale remains in balance, then the other B coin is the fake—if not, then the B coin on the scale is the fake and YOU HAVE SOLVED THE PROBLEM.

(c) If you have two A coins and one B coin left—as in either of the (iii) (b) scenarios—weigh the two A coins against each other. If the scale remains in balance, then the remaining B coin is the fake—if not, then the A coin which moves in the same direction as the original A pile is the fake and YOU HAVE SOLVED THE PROBLEM.

* At this point, you may be questioning the value of spending a significant amount of time struggling with a brain-buster like this final question if it doesn't directly help with school or exams. For many parents, this is a reasonable concern.

Reasonable, but, we would suggest, a little short-sighted.

The emphasis in many societies around the world on marks and positions has blinded parents to the real purpose of education—which is not, as we will demonstrate in the next volume, merely to pass some meaningless exams and be rated against how well everyone else can do in the same exam. The real purpose of education is to prepare us for whatever we might face in the future—a task for which the current school systems throughout the world are demonstrably unsuited.

To achieve this preparation, a young person (and his or her parents) must approach the training of the mind in the same way an Olympic athlete approaches training the body.

This involves a combination of two types of exercise:

• Low intensity, high repetition drills, which promote speed, agility and endurance, and train the 'muscle memory' for specific activities.

• High intensity, low repetition exercises which are far more demanding, but build strength and higher-level skills.

There are strong arguments for 'flying through' large numbers of relatively easy mental exercises of all kinds to create mental agility, endurance and automatic learning habits, and this is highly recommended.

However, the mind that is capable of the discipline of concentrating for an intense period on a brain-busting logic/lateral-thinking problem, and sticking at it until it gives up its solution, is one which will not 'crack' when the pressure is on. It has developed the mental 'muscle memory' for perseverance and tenacity, and, importantly, an understanding of the value of trial and error and learning from mistakes.

This is the mind of a future champion.

The creation of thinking individuals is not the exclusive (perhaps not even the primary) role of the education system—though in the 21st Century, it certainly should be! If more than half of our intelligence is the result of environmental factors, and 70 per cent—or more—of a child's time is spent outside of school, then the excuse, 'I just don't have the time to make a difference' is, except in the most extreme of circumstances, really only that: an excuse. What we choose to do with our time is our choice—no one else's—so the results we reap are ultimately our own responsibility. And though we can—and should!—find fault with the failings of 'the system', we should be equally rigorous in our assessment of the way we make use of the opportunities we ourselves have to really make a difference to our children.

GREAT MINDS, GREAT IDEAS

'We learn more by looking for the answer to a question and not finding it, than we do from learning the answer itself.' [51]

LLOYD ALEXANDER

Case Study 1

Maslow's Hierarchy of Needs

Maslow's eight-step hierarchy, which he refined over time, divides neatly into four 'Deficit Needs' and four 'Growth Needs'.

Deficit Needs:

1) Physiological Needs: hunger, thirst, bodily comforts, etc.
2) Safety/Security Needs: the elimination of danger (both physical and psychological)
3) Belonging and Love Needs: connection with others, being accepted
4) Esteem Needs: to achieve, be competent, gain approval and recognition (including self-esteem)

Growth Needs:

5) Cognitive Needs: to know, to understand and explore
6) Aesthetic Needs: symmetry, order and beauty
7) Self-Actualisation Needs: to find self-fulfilment and realise one's potential
8) Self-Transcendence Needs: to connect to something beyond the ego or to help others find self-fulfilment and realise their potential

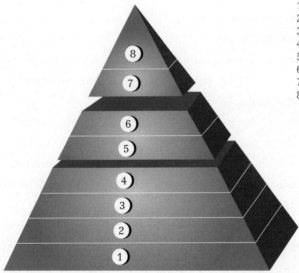

1. Physiological Needs
2. Safely Needs
3. Belonging & Love Needs
4. Esteem Needs
5. Need to Know & Understand
6. Aesthetic Needs
7. Self-Actualisation
8. Transcendence

This influential and eminently reasonable model has been strengthened in recent years by our increased understanding of the way the physical and neurological structures of the brain operate.

The influence of the more 'primitive' areas of the brain—particularly the ARAS (the Ascending Reticular Activating System) and the limbic system—in the creation of mindset, and our response to the surrounding environment, was covered in some detail in *Deeper than the Ocean*. The influence of these areas (especially the limbic system—the human 'emotion centre') helps explain the importance of the 'deficit needs' in Maslow's model, and reinforces the need for a child to feel safe and secure and accepted before any significant learning can take place.

As the more basic of our drives, the deficit needs (what Maslow called the 'D-Needs') must constantly be met, so these needs are continually shaping our children's behaviour and their readiness to achieve learning.

Deficit Needs

1. Physiological Needs

The physiological needs always take first precedence. They are those aspects which enable the human organism to function physically. From a survival—and therefore an evolutionary—point of view, a creature that does not instinctively safeguard its physical existence does not survive long enough to 'self-actualise' or even to reproduce. Physical survival is hard-wired into our brains, and takes precedence over all other drives or desires, so when some of these needs remain unmet, all other desires and capacities—especially the higher-order growth needs—are ruthlessly over-ridden.

Included in the physiological needs are breathing, eating and drinking, ridding the body of waste, sleeping, regulating body temperature, protecting the organism from disease and the drive for sexual activity.

Physiological needs are immediate and urgent, and act to inhibit the 'side-tracking' of attention into other areas, so in terms of learning and education—which relate more to the apex of the needs hierarchy—it is clear that should any of the physiological needs be lacking, the individual will have little or no drive to achieve in 'future-oriented' activities.

What this means for a parent or teacher is that a child who is hungry, sick, in pain, sleep-deprived or (in the case of adolescents) sexually preoccupied will have difficulty learning anything—which is hardly news to anyone.

2. Safety Needs

Once the physiological needs are met, safety and security outranks all other human needs, because in terms of survival potential, the need for safety is the next most urgent requirement of the human organism. Safety needs include physical security (from violence, aggression etc.); familial/relational security, moral and psychological security and health and material security (income, home environment etc.).

There is a certain amount of overlap between the first two levels of the 'Needs Pyramid', because at certain times, the need for safety—even psychological security—can, for short periods, outweigh even basic physiological drives. When running from the charging rhinoceros, we are unlikely to stop to pick a fruit to eat, no matter how hungry we might be!

A home (or social) environment that threatens the child's physical or even emotional security is, therefore, unlikely to be conducive to academic or educational success—even if the explicit reason for the 'threat' is to pressure the child into improving performance. It is important to remember that threat in this context does not necessarily mean the obvious fear of physical abuse. The prospect—overt or implied—of the withdrawal of approval is, in the context of the safety needs, a real threat.

A child coerced into studying harder by the threat of the physical, emotional or social consequences of failure is not working from the 'higher order' motivations of self-actualisation and growth, but rather in an attempt to address the deficit need of safety and love/belonging' (see the next section). The work will be task oriented and narrow in focus, and because the goal is survival and not growth, it is highly unlikely that the learning will be transferable to other areas of life, rendering the extra effort sterile.

On the other hand, a child who feels safe and secure no matter what results he/she might achieve, is far more likely to be working to address the 'higher needs', to learn with a forward-focussed mindset and to process in a way which leads to transferable learning.

3. Love/Belonging Needs

After the physiological and safety needs are satisfied, the human social needs are the next priority. The balance within this category of needs differs at different stages of life, but it always involves emotionally-based relationships such as friendship, sexual intimacy and/or family.

Human beings are gregarious creatures. They have a need to feel accepted—to 'fit in'—on an emotional level and this is particularly true during the period of adolescence, when the individual is still determining his/her position in relation to the world and other human beings.

Gangs, friendship groups, sporting teams, externally organised peer-groupings such as school classes, church groups etc.—and, of course, extended family—are all crucial, especially in the formative years. The need for love (both sexual and non-sexual) and acceptance is strong—certainly stronger than the desire to 'build a career' or 'lay down the foundations for a successful future'.

Understanding this allows parents—and teachers—to put many behaviours (and failings) into perspective. If these love/belonging elements are missing, or at risk, the likelihood of chronic loneliness, anxiety, even depression is significantly increased—especially in a negatively oriented environment such as the one created by the dominating mass media.

4. Esteem/Respect Needs

Esteem and respect—both fundamental deficit needs—are addressed through what psychologists call 'engagement' with society. Both involve received recognition in relation to activities to which the individual attaches some significance. To 'achieve' at a task/activity to which the individual attaches little or no importance promotes little self-esteem or self-respect, even if it promotes respect on the part of others (e.g. parents).

The importance of social/peer standing in the life—and particularly the mind—of the teen and pre-teen (and a good proportion of 'post-teens'!) can result in an over-sensitivity to the responses of others in areas which have assumed a level of personal significance; and, as they tend to be past- and present-oriented, rather than forward-looking, this sensitivity can tend to outweigh the growth needs.

Strategies for building self-esteem and self-respect—involving the recognition of real achievement, especially in areas which connect with the young person's personal values and beliefs—can help move him/her towards self-actualisation and Maslow's future-focussed levels of growth needs.

Growth Needs

The key difference between the growth needs and the needs outlined in the first four levels of the Needs Hierarchy lies in the fact that while deficit needs can be addressed and 'neutralised'—at least for a period—self-actualisation (leading to what Maslow and others refer to as 'self-transcendence') is an ongoing drive. Being future-oriented, self-actualisation (and even transcendence) is constantly evolving—with each achievement leading to the establishment of a new 'growth goal'. As Maslow put it, *'they are enduring motivations or drivers of behaviour.'* [52]

The other key difference between deficit needs and growth needs is that while deficit needs are focused inwards—on the needs and responses of the individual in relation to the environment—growth needs are focused outwards. They reach out towards understanding, appreciation and connection with the world beyond the self. This is why they are so pivotal in the development of growth and learning strategies.

If we can address the deficit needs so that their influence is diminished, we can actually employ the child's *need* to learn—to make sense of the world at a cognitive, aesthetic and self-actualising level. A child whose motivational drives are focussed outwards is primed for active understanding, which as we will demonstrate in Volume III, *The Art of Learning How to Learn,* is the key to effective learning.

5. Cognitive Needs

According to Maslow, the most basic of the growth needs in human beings is the need to understand; to gain knowledge and thus increase the ability to make connections—which as we have seen previously is the basis of creativity and intelligence. Cognitive needs involve learning, exploration, discovery, creativity, and a focus on detail.

Given the physiological basis of learning revealed by the discoveries of neuroscience, such drives are understandable, and increase 'survivability' in evolutionary terms.

6. Aesthetic Needs

Aesthetic appreciation is seen as a key step towards self-actualisation. Absorbing the beauty and pleasure that the world has to offer, ties the notion of cognitive understanding into the complex operations of the highly influential limbic system. It is part of the process of moving beyond the 'self' and establishing a mature connection with the 'otherness' of the world beyond.

7. Self-Actualisation

Maslow originally had only one level on his hierarchy above the four deficit needs—a level which he called self-actualisation. The four growth needs are a refinement of the key understanding that as human beings we have an intrinsic need to make the most of our abilities, and to strive to be the best we can be.

In the quotation which we used to open Part One, Section 2, Maslow wrote: *'Self-Actualisation is the intrinsic growth of what is already in the organism, or more accurately, of what the organism is.'*

Self-actualised people, according to Maslow's theory, possess certain key characteristics:

- Rather than denying or avoiding the facts and realities of the world (or themselves), they embrace them.
- They are objective and discerning in their outlook, weighing the pros and cons of issues and decisions.
- They are passionate and effective problem-solvers, both for themselves and for others.
- They exhibit spontaneity and creativity in their thoughts and actions.
- They tend to be empathetic and enjoy life.
- Their ethical and morality systems are intrinsic, rather than extrinsic (which means that their moral behaviour is based on their own decisions and structures, not on structures which are imposed from outside).

8. Self-Transcendence

Transcendence is a concept which has been recognised by the Positive Psychology movement as one of the key human virtues which exist throughout all cultures of the world. Simply stated, transcendence is the ability to recognise and embrace a larger purpose or existence than the mere personal.

Situated at the top of Maslow's hierarchy, self-transcendence is also sometimes referred to as 'Spiritual Needs'. As a gregarious creature, it is easy to see why this need might exist as a survival factor in the evolution of the human emotional system.

Individuals most likely to reach self-transcendence are self-actualising, mature, healthy and self-fulfilled.

Case Study 2

Jerome S. Bruner—Narrative and the 'Construction' of Reality

One of the great 20th Century thinkers in the area of cognitive and educational psychology, Jerome S. Bruner, argues that the 'cognitive revolution', fixated, as it is, on the mind as an 'information processor', has led psychology away from the more important purpose of understanding mind as a 'creator of meanings'.

In 1991, in a peer-reviewed journal called *Critical Inquiry*, Bruner published an article entitled 'The Narrative Construction of Reality'. This article argued that the mind structures and mediates its sense of reality through 'cultural products, like language and other symbolic systems'. He states that narrative is one of these key cultural products. 'Narrative', according to Bruner, consists of ten key elements:

- Narratives take place in relation to some notion of time.
- Narratives deal with events, though not all events are necessarily clear and defined—some events may well be left generalised and vague.
- Characters within a narrative are motivated and directed by 'beliefs, desires, theories, values, and so on'.
- Narratives store our interpretations of 'reality' through their role as an internally selected series of events constituting a 'story'.
- Stories are about something unusual happening that 'breaches' the character's (and, therefore, our own) 'normal' state.
- A narrative creates a reference (a way of interpreting) reality, although not in a direct way—the analogy is representative (symbolic) not literal.
- A narrative contains a generalisation which can be distilled from the particular events of the story—its 'representativeness'.
- Narrative implies a claim or an assumption about how one ought to act.
- Narrative, according to Bruner, assumes a relationship between author or text and reader, including the assigning of the reader's internal context to the narrative, and a willingness to 'suspend disbelief'—that is, to accept the events of the narrative, in the context of the narrative.
- Narratives (stories) are cumulative, that is, new stories exist in a context created by previously experienced ones.

In this discussion, narrative is not limited to literary products, like stories and plays, but is seen as a component in all our experiences.

Bruner observes that these ten characteristics describe both the narrative and the reality constructed and assumed by the narrative. Our concept of reality, therefore, is a construct of the human mind, which filters and structures sensory and emotional experience through the construction of narrative—what we refer to in Volume III, *The Art of Learning How to Learn*, as the 'narrative intelligence'.

Case Study 3

The Dual-Axis 'Ethical Spectrum' Model

In Part Two, Section 3, under the heading 'How to Refine Responsibility', we introduced the concept of an 'Ethical Spectrum' as a way of more objectively judging the ethical responsibility of any action. The position on the spectrum of any act measures its consequences on people other than the person making the decision. It is useful because of its simplicity in examining what is actually a complex set of human behaviours.

The 'Ethical Spectrum'

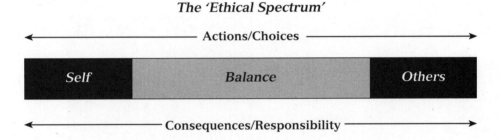

While this model offers an easy-to-interpret judgment of the ultimate consequences of an action, it is less effective in examining *intention* as a contributing element.

For young people, part of the process of training in ethical behaviour should include an awareness of the fact that though our intentions in committing to any particular action may be 'positive', this is no guarantee of its achieving favourable consequences for other people.

An awareness of this reality promotes a more considered approach to decision-making, and reduces the tendency to claim that 'the end justifies the means', which is often the beginning of a drift towards amoral or opportunistic decision-making, such as that which is often seen on the part of (for example) many elected politicians.

A young person who is able to examine the intention of an act (or an omission) before committing to a course of action is more likely to identify the possibility of negative consequences, which act against that original intention. Early training in the recognition of cause and effect, in all things, helps in the development of this aspect of ethical decision-making.

This Case Study presents a more sophisticated, two-axis model of the 'Ethical Spectrum'. This model separates the Result ('Action/Consequences') axis from the Intention ('Choices/Responsibility') axis.

The quadrants are labelled according to the balance between the relative positions of the act on the two axes. On both axes, the positive (+) direction indicates an action which has a favourable result (intended or actual) for others, while negative (-) indicates that the action is geared more towards 'self'.

It looks like this:

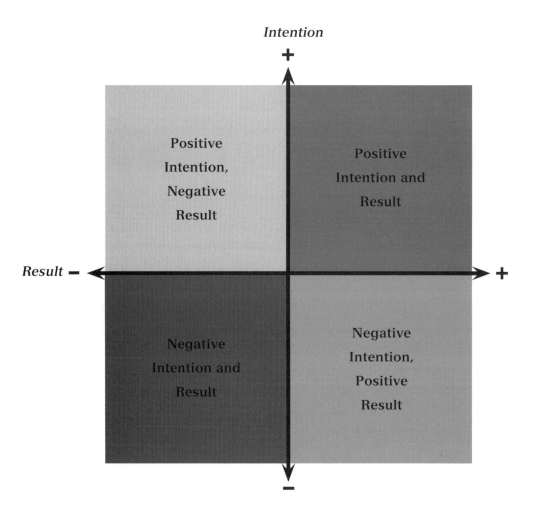

Consider the following scenarios:

1) Adam wants a new computer game but can't afford it, so he steals the money from his mother's purse, knowing that she is already short for the rent.

2) Alex saves the money for a new computer game, but on hearing that his mother is short for the rent, slips it into her purse instead.

3) Therese finds a wallet with $500 in it, and although the owner's i.d. is in the wallet, she takes the money and buys a present for her mother's birthday.

4) Tammy finds a wallet with $500 in it, and although the owner's i.d. is in the wallet, she takes the money and gives it to the poor, because they need it more.

5) Trish finds a wallet with $500 in it, and discovering that the owner's i.d. is in the wallet, she takes it to him, even though she has to catch a bus across town to do it.

6) Harry has volunteered to take his friends home from the city but he is late, so he breaks the speed limit to try to get there on time.

7) Barry breaks into a house to steal a TV, but discovers a girl tied up. She has been kidnapped. He frees her and helps her escape.

8) Billy breaks into a house to steal a TV, but discovers a girl tied up. She has been kidnapped. Afraid that he will be arrested for burglary, he leaves her there, but phones the police anonymously to tell them where she is.

9) Brad breaks into a house to steal a TV, but discovers a girl tied up. She has been kidnapped. Afraid that he will be arrested for burglary, he leaves her there and tells no one.

10) In a department store shopping for a present for his father, Tim knocks over a lamp and breaks it. If he pays for it, he won't be able to buy the present which his father really needs. He doesn't tell anyone, because the store is insured, so no one will lose.

The results might plot something like this:

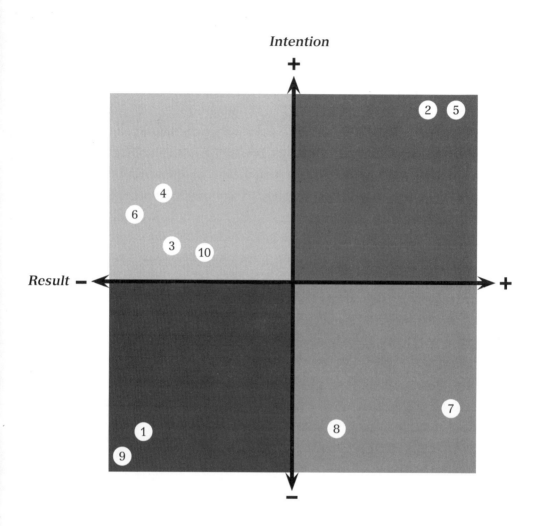

A discussion with a young person about where each of these—or a hundred similar situations—might fit on the model is really a discussion about relative ethics and indicates the young person's grasp of the 'Self/Other' concept of responsibility and ethical behaviour. Talking through the reasons for choosing a particular position is a good way of leading the young person to think more carefully through decisions—which is the beginning of 'responsible' decision-making.

The *Art* of **Communicating** *with your child*

REFERENCES

The following are some of the people, papers, books, articles and films mentioned in the preceding pages which we think are interesting, thought-provoking and/or informative. Most are very accessible, but some may be quite challenging. This is not intended to be a complete, comprehensive or thorough-going bibliography of the available information on the areas covered in this volume—the fields are simply too vast. Rather, it is a series of stepping-stones which should take you a little way out into the water, so that you can see further and follow up on any threads of insight which you find particularly interesting.

1. **(p 9) 'The voice of parents is the voice of gods...'**
   One of the Bard's many observations on the power of parenting. Though often-quoted, we have been unable to track down its original source.

2. **(p 17) 'Adults teach children in three important ways...'**
   Schweitzer lived his life by this rule—teaching not only children, but adults by his example.

3. **(p 18) 'Be yourself. Everyone else is already taken.'**
   Typical of Oscar Wilde's approach to life is this statement of his belief in individuality—a veiled comment on the pressure within Victorian society to conform.

4. **(p 19) 'If a child is to keep his inborn sense of wonder...'**
   Rachel Carson, *The Sense of Wonder* (1965), HarperCollins, 1998 (published posthumously).

5. **(p 21) 'When he was younger...'**
   From *My Life* STV12 (Singapore) November 1998.

6. **(p 21) 'I am grateful...'**
   Jeremy Lim, 'Don't Make Your Home Your Prison' in *TODAY* (Singapore) 3 November 2006.

7. **(p 21) 'Why is that baby so big...'**
   ibid

8. **(p 21) 'I thought...'**
   ibid

9. **(p 23) 'upsets into set-ups'**
   McKinsey's Michael Rennie, quoted in *What Makes a Champion!* Prof. Allan Snyder (ed), Penguin, Melbourne, 2002 (p 4).

10. (p 26) 'signal strengths...'

Seligman talks a lot of excellent sense about the 'signal strengths' in his outstanding book *Authentic Happiness* (London: Nicholas Brealey, 2003).

11. (p 26) 'Self Actualisation is the intrinsic growth...'

Maslow, writing in *Psychological Review*, 1949 and *Motivation and Personality,*1954.

12. (p 27) 'Your children need your presence more than your presents...'

As a minister, as well as a political activist, Jesse Jackson sees the breakdown of family structures as one of the key factors in the growth of social problems—as this quote shows.

13. (p 28) 'the study of crippled, stunted, immature...'

Maslow wrote this in *Motivation and Personality* (1954).

14. (p 29) 'I believe what really happens in history is this...'

This Chesterton gem, and many others, can be found in *What's Wrong with the World* (1910). It is typical of his incisive observation of human foibles, and his ability to force us to look at—and laugh at—ourselves.

15. (p 30) 'The children today love luxury...'

Though none of the written works of Socrates survive, we know of his teachings through the writings of his students and contemporaries. This analysis of Athenian youth has always been attributed to him.

16. (p 30) 'I see no hope for the future of our people...'

Though not a part of any of his great poems, this observation is always attributed to Hesiod.

17. (p 31) 'The world is passing through troubled times...'

Apart from leading an ill-fated crusade, Peter the Hermit was famous as an orator (which is probably how he raised his army in the first place). This gem is taken from one of his more memorable sermons, delivered in 1274 AD.

18. (p 32) 'When I was a boy of fourteen, my father was so ignorant...'

Twain made this wonderfully ironic observation in *Old Times on the Mississippi* in the *Atlantic Monthly*, 1874.

19. (p 35) 'I know that you believe you understand what you think I said...'

A classic piece of diplomatic language from a career diplomat!

20. (p 40) 'Titanic...'

20th Century Fox movie directed by James Cameron, this film holds an impressive number of records—including most Oscar nominations (14), most Oscar wins (11), highest box-office take and most weeks at number one (15).

21. **(p 42) 'Habit is habit...'**

Often quoted by inspirational speakers and people advising on 'How to Quit...' this wisdom is taken from *Mark Twain's Notebook* posthumously published (in 1935).

22. **(p 47) 'Children have never been very good at...'**

Baldwin's remark is one whose essential truth most parents discover eventually—often to their severe embarrassment.

23. **(p 50) 'Children are so unpredictable...'**

An accurate observation of one of the pitfalls of parenthood, attributed to Franklin P Jones (1887–1929) a US businessman with a famous and oft-quoted wit.

24. **(p 60) 'You yourself, as much as anybody...'**

This inspiring quote has always been attributed to Buddha.

25. **(p 61) 'Dignity does not consist in possessing honours...'**

More wisdom from the author of *The Nicomachean Ethics* (c. 325 BC).

26. **(p 62) 'footless self-esteem...'**

This was a phrase used by Seligman in a 2006 lecture to members of the Australian Psychological Society, attended by one of the authors.

27. **(p 71) 'As adults, we must ask more of our children...'**

From *The Art of the Possible: A Compassionate Approach to Understanding the Way People Learn, Think and Communicate*. By Dawna Markova (1991).

28. **(p 72) 'Don't worry that your children never listen to you...'**

From *All I Really Need to Know I Learned in Kindergarten* by Robert Fulghum (1986).

29. **(p 74) 'The best brought-up children...'**

Shaw included this advice under the heading 'Maxims for Revolutionists' in the published version of *Man and Superman*.

30. **(p 74) 'If there is anything that we wish to change...'**

This wisdom, and much more, can be found in Jung's seminal work *Vom Werden der Persönlichkeit* (On the Development of Personality), first published in 1932.

31. **(p 75) 'We need to keep their limitations in mind...'**

Dr Monica Luciana, from a study into teenagers' abilities to multi-task in *Child Development*, May/June 2005 issue.

32. **(p 77) 'Societies that provide infants...'**

This quote and the next one are taken from the paper 'Body Pleasure and the

Origins of Violence' by James W. Prescott. For a full text of this fascinating article, visit http://www.scireview.de/prescott/article.html

33. **(p 77) 'pleasure and violence have a reciprocal relationship...'**
ibid

34. **(p 82) 'Champions are often familiar with adversity...'**
From *What Makes a Champion!* (Penguin, Melbourne, 2002) Edited by Professor Allan Snyder (p4).

35. **(p 87) 'The greatest remedy for anger is delay...'**
Seneca's early experience was in the Roman law-courts. Perhaps this philosophy grew up there.

36. **(p 90) 'The only fault's with time...'**
Lines from Browning's play *Luria*.

37. **(p 92) 'It is reasonable to speculate that teenagers...'**
To read the full text of this paper, go to:
http://serendip.brynmawr.edu/bb/neuro/neuro05/web2/kcheng.html

38. **(p 102) 'It is better to bind your children to you...'**
As a former Roman slave, Terence understood the difference between demanding authority and earning respect.

39. **(p 103) 'If you want children to keep their feet on the ground...'**
One of the more memorable and useful pieces of advice from the world's most famous advice columnist—Dear Abby.

40. **(p 104) 'Anger blows out the lamp of the mind...'**
From Ingersoll's book *Some Reasons Why*. Project Gutenberg has just released volume VIII of *The Works of Robert G. Ingersoll*. It is a free download and can be accessed at http://www.gutenberg.org/etext/20447.

41. **(p 105) 'Anybody can become angry...'**
We have not been able to find the original source for this quote, but it is generally accepted to have been one of Aristotle's.

42. **(p 106) 'You cannot,' she said...**
This is a sadly ironic quote, considering the manner of Indira Gandhi's death not long after she said this. She was assassinated by her own bodyguards.

43. **(p 111) 'In Nature, there are neither rewards nor punishments...'**
Another quote from *Some Reasons Why* (See above Reference 40).

44. (p 117) 'Rather than teaching our children...'

Miki Kanamaru, from a wide-ranging and extremely helpful conversation with the authors in 2006.

45. (p 118) 'the wages of Sin is Death...'

St Paul's dire warning can be found in the Bible (Romans 6:23).

46. (p 119) 'How unhappy is he who cannot forgive himself...'

One of many pearls of wisdom to be found in Publilius Syrus' *Sententiae* (circa 42 BC).

47. (p 126) 'Live so that when your children think of fairness...'

From *Life's Little Treasure Book on Parenting* by H. Jackson Brown, Rutlidge Hill Press (1995).

48. (p 130) 'we have the power to [consciously] shape our brains...'

From *The Mind & the Brain—Neuroplasticity and the Power of Mental Force* (2002) by Jeffrey M. Schwartz and Sharon Begley—a fascinating account of one man's work in the area of conscious brain formation.

49. (p 132) 'Too often we give children answers...'

Insightful words from psychiatrist Roger Lewin in his book *Compassion*.

50. (p 137) 'Backwards understood be only can but...'

This is Kierkegaard having fun with a famous quote from Goethe, which ran: 'Life can only be understood backwards, but it must be lived forwards.'

51. (p 152) 'We learn more by looking for...'

As a writer for young people for over half a century, Lloyd Alexander understood the value of stretching their imaginations.

52. (p 157) 'they are enduring motivations or drivers of behaviour...'

From *Psychological Review*, 1949.

GLOSSARY

Abstract Thought/Reasoning

[From the Latin 'ab-' (away) and 'trahere' (to draw)] The ability to consider an idea or concept apart from concrete matter or specific examples, including the ability to mentally construct a logical sequence of cause and effect.

Active Learning/Recall

Learning and recalling with understanding (as opposed to 'rote' or 'drill' learning, which is memorisation without understanding of the underlying principles or concepts). Active understanding involves the association of novel material with previously existing knowledge, to synthesise the 'new' understanding.

ad hoc

[Latin for 'for one particular purpose; especially']

Amygdala

[From the Greek 'amygdale' (almond) for its shape] Known as the seat of emotion, the amygdala is part of the limbic system (the 'mammalian brain'). Its actions are reflexive, responding to changes in the surrounding environment—especially those which spell danger. Many human psychological disorders and the inappropriate social responses of young people can be traced back to an overactive (or inappropriately stimulated) amygdala, or an overdependence on its processing functions (especially during the period of life before the pre-frontal cortex is fully developed).

Analogy

[From the Greek 'analogos' (proportion)] A comparison which emphasises elements in one case, by demonstrating similar elements in another (cf: metaphor).

ARAS (Ascending Reticular Activating System)/Reticular Formation

[From the Latin 'rete' (net)—because of its appearance—but appropriate, ironically, for its wide-ranging functional reach] Situated at the core of the brain-stem but extending upwards into areas in the thalamus, hypothalamus and cortex and downwards to the cerebellum and the sensory nerves, the reticular formation is involved in semi-automatic actions, such as walking, sleeping and lying down and as many as 25 different physical activities. As such, it is absolutely essential for any form of conscious life. Recent study of this complex formation strongly suggests that its role in our conscious (and non-conscious) decision-making and our internalisation of the environment surrounding us are equally important.

Association/Associative
[From the Latin *'associatio'* (root: *'socius'*—sharing, allied)] In psychological terms, association refers to the connecting of ideas—especially the linking of new input with previously learned information—to create a new understanding.

Axon
[Greek for 'axis'] A nerve-fibre (part of the neuron—often called a nerve-cell) responsible for carrying information in the form of electrical impulses away from the cell body to communicate it to another cell (or cells).

Brainstorm/ Mindmap/ Ideagram
A non-linear ideation aid which mimics the unstructured nature of the non-conscious imagination by noting down random ideas as they are generated, without prioritisation. Usually drawn in the form of a central circle, with spiral arms.

Cognition
[From the Latin *'co-'* (together) and *'(g)nosere'* (to know)] All the processes by which the sensory input is transformed, reduced, elaborated, stored, recovered and used.

Cognitive Psychology
[From the Latin *'co-'* (together) and *'(g)nosere'* (to know) and the Greek *'psukhe'*—*'psyche'*—(soul or mind—from the maiden in Greek mythology, who is the personification of the human soul)] The branch of psychology which studies cognition, the mental processes (thinking, reasoning, decision-making, association—even emotions) which result in behaviour. It is a wide-ranging discipline, studying perception, memory, reasoning, problem-solving, creativity and many other areas.

Concept

[From the Latin *'conceptus'* (conceive)] A general notion, a generalisation.

Corpus Callosum

[From the Latin *'corpus'* (body) and *'callosum'* (callous), literally 'calloused body'—a reference to its appearance] The fibrous 'bridge' of axons which links the two hemispheres of the brain, facilitating cooperative 'communication' between them.

Creativity Theory

[From the Latin *'creare'* (bring into existence)] The name given to a group of conceptualised structures describing the operation of human creativity.

Domain(s)

[From the Latin *'dominus'* (lord)] A distinct field of thought, action or study.

Duchenne Smile

Named after Guillaume Duchenne, the french anatomist who first described it, the Duchenne smile is an authentic or genuine smile, in which the corners of the mouth turn up and the skin around the corners of your eyes crinkles. An inauthentic smile tends not to make it up as far as the eyes. The non-conscious is very adept at picking the difference and setting up an emotional reaction accordingly, without input from the conscious.

Frontal Lobes

[From the Greek *'lobos'* (rounded)] Situated at the front end of each cerebral hemisphere, the frontal lobes play a significant role in judgment, the control of impulse, language, motor function, problem-solving, memory, socialisation, sexual behaviour and spontaneous responses. The frontal lobes assist in the planning, coordinating, controlling and executing of behaviour.

Functional Magnetic Resonance Imaging (fMRI)

Magnetic Resonance Imaging (MRI), originally known as Nuclear Magnetic Resonance Imaging (NMRI), relies on understanding the predictable effect of a strong magnetic field on the excited hydrogen nuclei of water molecules within a structure (like the human brain, for example). This effect can be measured using sophisticated tomography [from the Greek *tomos* (slice) and *graphia* (describing)]—a computer-based 3-D imaging process—to build an accurate three-dimensional picture of the internal structure of the object.

Functional MRI (fMRI) technology was developed to measure the haemodynamic response (the changes in blood flow and blood oxygenation within the brain) which occurs when neural activity takes place in a specific part of the brain. By targeting the imaging process and applying it to specific brain activities, researchers have been able to accurately pinpoint the areas of the brain which are activated during specific cognitive events.

Gestalt

[From the German *'gestalt'* (form, state)] An organised whole in which each individual part affects every other, the whole being more than the sum of its parts.

Hierarchy

[From the Greek *'hieros'* (sacred) and *'arkhes'* (ruler)] Any graded organisation. It derives from the three divisions of angels in the Bible.

Ideation

[From the Latin *'idea'* (form)] Imagining, conceiving or forming ideas, usually through a process of internal association or synthesis of existing knowledge and novel input.

Ideagram (See Brainstorm)

Limbic System

[From the Latin *'limbus'* (arc) which describes its curved shape] The collective name for the human—and mammalian—brain structures controlling emotion, motivation and emotional association with memory, the limbic system influences the formation of memory by integrating emotional states with stored memories of accompanying physical sensations. This is a key survival attribute which has been passed down, allowing an instantaneous response to danger—unfettered by the slower, if more reasoned, cognitive processes.

Lobe(s)

[From the Greek 'lobos' (rounded)] Divisions of the brain. In each hemisphere of the human brain, there are four main lobes: the frontal lobe, the parietal lobe, the occipital lobe and the temporal lobe.

Frontal: The most recently developed—and advanced—region of the cortex in evolutionary terms, the frontal lobes are the 'advanced programmeming and control modules' of the human super-computer. They are responsible for planning, integrating information and maintaining executive control of cognitive functions, abstract reasoning, conscious association, judgment (including moral and ethical), wisdom, ambition and our conscious awareness of 'self'.

In human beings, the frontal lobes are the last area of the brain to come 'online'—only fully developing their functions in the early twenties. This fact is important when we analyse the sometimes erratic behaviour and reactions of adolescents and teenagers, whose rapid development in other areas of cognitive activity is not matched by the growth of these key 'control centres'.

Each frontal lobe is further divided into:

- The anterior (front) portion of the frontal lobe, called the prefrontal cortex. It is very important for the 'higher cognitive functions' and the determination of the personality.
- The posterior (back) portion of the frontal lobe. This consists of the premotor and motor areas. Nerve cells that produce movement are located in the motor areas. The premotor areas serve to modify movements.

Occipital: These are the primary visual reception areas of the brain. They are also the primary visual association areas. This means that they process the initial image and have the capacity for visual interpretation (later refined within the frontal cortex).

In computing terminology, they are the processor for the scanner and/or the digital camera, involved in 'acquiring and storing' visual images.

Parietal: The 'virtual reality modules' of the brain, the parietal lobes are concerned with the assimilation of sensory input, sensory discrimination, body orientation and primary and secondary somatic processing [From the Greek 'soma' (body)]. In simple terms, their job is to create a sense of the three-dimensional layout of the external world, and the existence of your own body in relation to that spatial layout.

Temporal: Just as the occipital lobes are concerned primarily with vision, the temporal lobes—the brain's 'media player and word processor'—are largely concerned with hearing. They are the auditory reception and association areas. They are also involved in expressed behaviour, language assimilation, speech, memory retrieval, emotion and some more advanced aspects of perception.

Mensa

Mensa is the largest, oldest, and best-known high-IQ society in the world, restricting membership to people with testable IQs within the top 2 per cent of any approved standardised intelligence test.

Metaphor

[From the Greek *'metaphora'* (transfer)] A comparison which assigns a name of attribute to an object to which it is not literally applicable. (eg: The Dragon of room 2C. for a feared teacher).

Mindmap (See Brainstorm)
Mindset

[From the Latin *'mens'* (mind) and the Old English *'settan'* (sit)] The existing mental framework against which each of us judges any new experience. This template is subject to constant change, as it is 'upgraded' by events and observations, but the human tendency (fuelled by the actions of the ARAS) to reinforce and focus on the expected means that the experiences which are influencing the evolution of the individual's mindset are themselves being moderated—or selectively altered—by the existing template.

Mindset Environment

[From the Latin *'mens'* (mind) and the Old English *'settan'* (sit) and theOld French *'viron'* (circuit, neighbourhood)] The elements of a person's existing perception of the world and his/her relationship with the surrounding environment, which affects or influences his/her perception of reality.

Modelling

[From the French 'modèle' (example)] In psychology and education, modelling refers to the development of a skill through the emulation or imitation of an example or model.

Multi-tasking

[From the Latin 'mullus' (many) and 'tasca' (tax)] Originally a computing term referring to the simultaneous performance of two or more tasks by a computer's CPU (Central Processing Unit), multi-tasking is now a more universal term for the ability to manage the demands of multiple tasks simultaneously—a talent which, anecdotally, more women are suited to than men.

Neural (or Synaptic) Pruning

[From the Greek 'neuron' (a sinew)] A chemical process that reduces the number of connections within the brain. An intense period of neural pruning takes place between the ages of approximately twelve and twenty-two until the number of neural connections reaches a number which will remain basically stable for the rest of the person's life. The fact that the connections which tend to be pruned are those which are not myelinated has suggested that the process is one of 'use it or lose it'—or Neural Darwinism—a term which originated with Gerald Edelman's book *Neural Darwinism: The Theory of Neuronal Group Selection* (1987).

Neuron(s)/Neural

[From the Greek 'neuron' (a sinew)] Sometimes called nerve cells, though this term is not entirely correct as many neurons do not form nerves, they are found in the brain, the spinal cord and in the nerves and ganglia of the peripheral nervous system. Neurons process and transmit neural information. An important characteristic of neurons is that they have excitable membranes that allow them to generate and propagate electrical signals.

Neuroplasticity

[Also referred to as 'cortical plasticity', from the Greek 'cortex' (bark or rind) and 'plastikos' (moldable)]. The changes that occur in the organisation of the brain, particularly at the location of specific information processing functions, as a result of learning and experience. Though 'plasticity' is more evident in young children, there is no scientific reason to believe that once a brain injury occurs, there is little that can repair the damage. Often, repeated practice of an action or process can induce the formation of neural networks supporting that process in a region or area of the brain not normally associated with that particular process.

Neuroscience/Neurology
[From the Greek *'neuron'* (a sinew) and the Latin *'scire'* (to know)] The branch of medicine (and science) concerned with the study of nerves, the brain and the nervous system.

Neuro-Transmitters
[From the Greek *'neuron'* (a sinew) and the Latin *'trans-'* (a prefix meaning 'across', 'beyond') and *'mittere'* (send)] Chemicals produced in the axon of the presynaptic neuron (the neuron 'transmitting' the information) to relay, amplify and modulate electrical signals between a neuron and another cell. The neurotransmitter binds to receptors facing into the synapse from the dendrite or *soma* (cell-body) of the postsynaptic cell (the one 'receiving' the information).

Non-conscious
[From the Latin *'non'* (not) and *'conscius'*—derived from *'scire'* (to know)] (Often used interchangeably with subconscious—a term which is not as all-encompassing, as it generally does not refer to the autonomic functions and operations which are included in our usage of the term 'non-conscious') The portion of cognitive and lower mental activity not directly accessible to the conscious awareness, but sometimes susceptible to recall after the event.

Optimal Flow Method™
[From the Latin *'optimus'* (best)] A principle of organizing information—especially curriculum content—in a brain-friendly 'narrative-flow', which allows the narrative intelligence to place each element into a sequential context, thus 'fast-tracking' expertise (as defined in Cognitive Load Theory), by creating meaning that connects with a matrix of existing knowledge. Created by the authors.

Polymath (Polyhistor)
[From the Greek *'polys'* (many; great in number) and *'manthanein'* (to learn) and

'histos' (web; tissue)] A person of great and varied (encyclopaedic) learning. Often referred to as a 'Renaissance Intellectual' in honour of the great thinkers of that period—most notably Leonardo da Vinci, who excelled in a variety of areas from the arts to mathematics, athletics and the sciences. The 'math' segment of the term does not relate to whether the person has any connection to mathematics. The term 'polymath' is often used to describe those who excel in both the arts and sciences. Many highly accomplished people cannot be classed as polymaths as they worked solely in one field. People with the widest range of knowledge are also known as polyhistors. A polyglot is someone who is competent in a number of different languages.

Pre-Frontal Cortex—See Lobe(s).

Quantum Physics/Quantum Mechanics
[From the Latin *'quantus'* (how much)] One of the two pillars (along with Relativity) of modern physics, quantum physics/mechanics is an explanation of the behaviour of matter and energy at atomic and subatomic levels—where the laws of classical physics and electromagnetism break down. Based on quantum theory—the theory that energy is not a smoothly-flowing continuum but is manifested by emissions from radiating bodies of discrete particles or quanta—it is a theoretical discipline, whose mathematical principles underpin many areas of modern physics and chemistry.

Random Access Memory (RAM)
In computing, RAM generally denotes the active or working memory of a computer, but it actually refers to any data storage format and equipment that allow the stored data to be accessed in any order—that is, at random, not just in sequence, as is the case with other types of memory devices such as magnetic tapes, which can access data only in a predetermined order due to limitations of their mechanical design.

Relativity Theory
[From the Latin *'relativus'* (relate) and the Greek *'theoria'* (to behold)] Proposed by Einstein between 1905 (when he introduced the Special Theory of Relativity) and 1915 (between 1907 and 1915, he was working on a General Theory to work out

anomalies in the Special Theory), Relativity Theory overturned many of the tenets of traditional (Newtonian) physics.

It is based on the principle that all motion is relative, regarding space-time as a four dimensional continuum.

Virtually incomprehensible in its entirety to non-physicists, it is famous for a few key concepts: that time is not a constant, but alters relative to movement; that two events which appear to be simultaneous to a stationary observer are not simultaneous to another observer, moving relative to the first; that mass and energy are equivalent and transmutable (that is they can be converted from one state to the other—which is the meaning of the famous equation $E=mc^2$, which was used to develop the concept of nuclear energy—and nuclear weapons) and that space-time is curved, explaining the observed actions of gravity.

Confused? So was the world and the scientific community when Einstein—soon to become the universal symbol of the human capacity for genius—first proposed his world-changing ideas. Even a century later, few can get their heads around his amazing conceptualisation.

Schema
[From the Greek *'skhema'* (synopsis)] A general notion, a generalisation.

Self-Actualisation
[From the Old German *'selb'* (self) and the Latin *'actualis'* (real)] Self-actualisation is the instinctual need of humans (and, according to some theories, all creatures) to make the most of their inbuilt potential and to strive to be the best they can.

Synapse
[From the Greek *'syn'* (together) and *'hapsis'* (a joining)] The 'gap' across which the signals from the axon of one neuron cross (with the aid of neuro-transmitters) to the dendrite or the cell-body of another.

Synaptogenesis/Synaptic Proliferation
[A combination of synapse (see above) and (a) the Greek *'genesis'* (origin) and (b) the Latin *'prolis'* (offspring) and *'ferre'* (to bear)] Sometimes inaccurately referred to as 'neural proliferation', synaptic proliferation, also called synaptogenesis, is a genetically-controlled physical process in which neurons form connections

with a network of other neurons through the growth and branching of axons and dendrites.

Thalamus

[From the Greek 'thalamos' (chamber)] Located at the base of the brain, the thalamus is part of the limbic system and is the chief centre for the transmission of sensory impulses to the cerebral cortex. It is sometimes called the brain's 'switchboard'.

Visualisation

[From the Latin 'videre' (to see); 'visus' (sight)] The act of forming a visual image—hence the word 'imagination'. Often used to denote the mental rehearsal of a desired result.

PERSONALITIES

Alexander, Lloyd Chudley

(1924–2007) US author of more than forty books, mostly fantasy novels. Lloyd Alexander wrote mainly for children and adolescents, though he did publish some adult books. His most famous contribution to children's literature was the award-winning fantasy series *The Chronicles of Prydain*. Among other achievements, Lloyd Alexander was awarded, the prestigious Newbery Medal, the National Book Award and the American Book Award.

Aristotle

(384–322 BC) Greek philosopher and polymath during the golden age of Athens. He was influenced by Socrates and Plato. Aristotle laid the foundation for empirical scientific method, mentored Alexander the Great and taught and wrote on such diverse topics as biology and zoology, logic and rhetoric, physics, poetry and government.

Braddock, James J. (James Walter)

(1905–1974) US heavyweight boxing champion. Braddock fought under the name James J. Braddock as a homage to the great boxer James J Corbett. After breaking his hand in a fight and enduring a punishing career slump, then retiring from the ring to support his family, during the Great Depression, by working on the docks, Braddock made a legendary comeback which earned him the nickname 'The Cinderella Man'. This was also the name of the film biography, directed by Ron Howard and starring Russell Crowe in the title role.

Briñol, Pablo

Pablo Briñol received his Ph.D in 1999 from Universidad Autonoma Madrid under the supervision of Richard E. Petty and Alberto Becerra. Since then, he has been an Assistant Professor in the Social Psychology Department there, and continues developing his research with Professor Petty at Ohio State University. His research interests focus on the study of attitude change.

Brown, H. Jackson

US author, best-known for his book *Life's Little Instruction Book* which was on the New York Times bestseller list for 158 weeks. Beginning as the creative director of an advertising agency, Brown began writing books based on words of wisdom gathered from other people and his own experiences. His 33 books have been translated into 35 languages, and have sold millions of copies worldwide.

Browning, Robert

(1812–1889) A British poet and playwright whose mastery of dramatic verse, especially dramatic monologues, made him one of the foremost Victorian poets. His love affair and marriage (against her powerful family's wishes) to Elizabeth Barrett Browning (a talented poet in her own right) was one of the most famous literary relationships ever chronicled.

Bruner, Jerome S.

(1915–) A US constructivist psychologist whose areas of contribution include cognitive psychology and cognitive learning theory in educational psychology and to the general philosophy of education. Bruner is currently a senior research fellow at the New York University School of Law.

Bruner's ideas are based on categorisation—a belief that he summarised with the following: *'To perceive is to categorise, to conceptualise is to categorise, to learn is to form categories, to make decisions is to categorise.'* Bruner maintains people interpret the world in terms of its similarities and differences—and in terms of cultural and narrative structures.

Buddha (Siddhartha Gautama)

(Traditionally 563–483 BC, recently revised to circa 480–400 BC) Religious leader from ancient India/Nepal and the historical founder of Buddhism. 'Buddha' literally means 'enlightened one', and refers to any being which has permanently overcome greed, ignorance and anger, and has achieved Nirvana—which is total liberation from suffering.

Carson, Rachel Louise

(1907–1964) US writer, scientist, and ecologist. Rachel Carson spent much of her life campaigning for the environment, and was instrumental in leading the fight against the overuse of chemical pesticides such as DDT. She became a target of the powerful chemical companies who tried hard to discredit her, but her campaign was ultimately successful. She is considered one of the spiritual founders of the modern environmentalist movement and the Environmental Protection Agency. She was awarded the Presidential Medal of Freedom posthumously.

Chesterton, G.K. (Gilbert Keith)

(1874–1936) Influential English writer of the early 20th Century. He wrote in a variety of diverse genres, including detective fiction, fantasy, poetry, philosophy, journalism, biography and Christian apologetics. Chesterton is famous for his wit and his clever aphorisms, such as: *'Too much capitalism does not mean too many capitalists, but too few capitalists.'*

This statement is representative of his belief in the political philosophy known as Distributism—which was also favoured by influential writer and philosopher Hilaire Belloc. This philosophy, strongly supported by the 'social justice encyclicals' of the Catholic Church (to which Chesterton was a convert), called for the ownership of the means of production being spread as widely as possible among the population of the country, rather than the state-controlled socialist model, or the 'regency of the rich', which epitomised capitalism.

Clarke, Ronald (Ron) William

(1937–) Australian athlete, and one of the best known middle and long distance runners in the 1960s. He is best remembered for setting seventeen world records. As a promising 19-year-old, he was chosen to light the Olympic Flame in the stadium during the opening ceremonies of the 1956 Summer Olympics in Melbourne. He was elected Mayor of the Gold Coast, Queensland, in 2004.

Collette, Toni (Antonia)

(1972–) Academy Award-nominated Australian character actress and musician, best known for her roles in the films *The Sixth Sense, Muriel's Wedding, In Her Shoes* and *Little Miss Sunshine*. She has won four Australian Film Industry Awards.

Da Vinci, Leonardo

(1452–1519) Italian polymath, painter, sculptor, architect, musician, engineer, inventor and scientist. The epitome of the Renaissance intellectual, Da Vinci is considered by most commentators to be the greatest—or at least one of the top three—genius of all time. His influence on European thought in any number of areas is impossible to measure. His creations—such as the *Mona Lisa* and *The Last Supper*—are iconic, and his ability to make connections between previously unrelated elements from vastly different domains represents the essence and the epitome of human creativity.

Dahl, Roald

(1916–1990) British novelist, short story author and screenwriter of Norwegian parentage, famous as a writer for both children and adults.

His most popular children's books include Charlie and the Chocolate Factory, James and the Giant Peach, Matilda, The Witches and The BFG. He wrote only two novels for adults, but published fifteen books of short stories (including Kiss, Kiss, and Tales of the Unexpected—which gave rise to a television mystery series) and some non-fiction (including his autobiography, Boy).

Darwin, Charles

(1809–1882) British naturalist. Following his five year voyage on *The Beagle*—notably to the remote Galapagos Islands—Darwin developed his theory of 'Evolution Through Natural and Sexual Selection' (often called 'Natural Selection' or 'Darwinism' or simply 'Evolution'). This theory (though it has many vocal detractors) is the central paradigm around which most biological study is now based and has been strengthened by discoveries in the diverse areas of archaeology, comparative anatomy and genetics.

Duchenne, Guillaume Benjamin Amand

(1806–1875) French neurologist, the first scientist to describe several nervous and muscular disorders. In developing medical treatment for them, he created the fields of electrotherapy and electrodiagnosis. Duchenne applied electrodes for recording the path that electricity took in a contracting muscle's fibres, investigating every major superficial muscle. In the course of 'mapping' 100 facial muscles in 1862, he observed that false, or even half-hearted, smiles involved only muscles of the mouth, while genuine (Duchenne) smiles also activate the *pars lateralis* muscle around the eyes. Duchenne is also credited with pioneering a technique which he called 'harpooning', which is seen as the forerunner of the modern biopsy.

Edelman, Gerald Maurice

(1929–) US neuroscientist, immunologist, biological chemist and Nobel Laureate. Famous for his biomolecular work in defining the chemical composition of antibodies, his work in the area of neuroscience is equally ground-breaking, focussing on what he calls 'neural Darwinism', the theory that populations of neurons develop individual networks through a Darwinian selection process (rather than being pre-programmemed purely by genetics). Edelman proposes a comprehensive multidisciplinary 'unification' theory of consciousness, integrating anatomy, brain composition and structure, neural connectivity, cell biology and psychology. From the cognitive point of view, this work presents an ambitious 'unified theory' embracing the actions of perception, memory, learning, language, and consciousness as we understand them.

Einstein, Albert

(1879–1955) German-born theoretical physicist regarded as the most important scientist of the 20th Century. His name is synonymous with the notion of genius and intelligence—a status enhanced by the seemingly endless array of aphorisms (short, pithy and insightful observations) on many subjects, which have come down to us from the great man's mind. Einstein's Special and General Theories of Relativity redefined the way the world looks at physical structure, time and energy. He was a leading player in the development of quantum mechanics, modern theories of gravitation and cosmology, and his famous formulation $E=mc^2$ was the insight which, in other hands, led to the development of nuclear power and nuclear weaponry—a development which Einstein, the humanitarian, bitterly regretted.

Frost, Robert

(1874–1963) US poet and teacher and four-time Pulitzer Prize winner. Frost is one of America's most beloved and respected poets. His works are studied worldwide for their eloquent simplicity and insight.

Fulghum, Robert

(1937–) American minister, teacher and author, primarily of short essays. A multi-talented man (he is an accomplished artist and sculptor, and a musician), he came to prominence in 1986 with his first collection, *All I Really Need to Know I Learned in Kindergarten*, which stayed on the New York Times bestseller lists for nearly two years.

Gandhi, Indira Priyadarshini

(1917–1984) Indian politician. The daughter of Jawaharlal Nehru, India's first post-independence Prime Minister, she was the Prime Minister of India for three consecutive terms from 1966 to 1977 and for a fourth term from 1980 until her assassination in 1984.

Gandhi was a consummate politician, who could outmanoeuvre opponents through populism to win elections. She introduced less conservative economic policies and promoted agricultural productivity in India, but her handling of internal dissent—especially the separatist movement in Punjab, finally led to her assassination in 1984 at the hands of her own bodyguards.

Goethe, Johann Wolfgang von

(1749–1832) German novelist, dramatist, poet, painter, humanist, scientist, philosopher, and for ten years chief minister of state at Weimar. A polymath in the mould of Da Vinci, Goethe was a key figure in German art and literature (influencing Classicism, Enlightenment, Sturm und Drang and Romanticism). He was also influential in scientific circles, influencing Charles Darwin among others. Goethe's thinking reverberated through European arts and philosophy for over a century, and the influences are still felt today.

Grossberg, Stephen

US academic specialising in cognitive and neural systems, mathematics, psychology and biomedical engineering. Grossberg is one of the principal founders of the fields of computational neuroscience, connectionist cognitive science and artificial neural network research. He is also a member of the 'modern scientific movement', developing a model for how the brain works—how it sees, learns, recognises and keeps track of objects, memories and complex situations. These overlapping fields of research have led to the technically sophisticated Adaptive Resonance Theory (ART) of neural architecture.

Hawkins, Jeff

(1957–) US inventor, researcher and author. Founder of Palm Computing and inventor of the Palm Pilot, Hawkins now works full-time in the area of neuroscience. His book *On Intelligence: How a New Understanding of the Brain will Lead to the Creation of Truly Intelligent Machines* (New York: Times Books, 2004) outlines his groundbreaking Memory Prediction Framework.

Hayes, Rutherford B. (Birchard)

(1822–1893) US politician, lawyer, military leader and the nineteenth President of the United States (1877–1881). Hayes was elected President by one electoral vote after the highly disputed election of 1876, when he lost the popular vote to his opponent, Samuel Tilden.

Hesiod

(circa 700 BC) An early Greek poet, Hesiod along with Homer, with whom Hesiod is often paired, are the earliest Greek poets whose work has survived. Modern scholars disagree as to which was earlier because both lived centuries before recorded history, but Hesiod's writings serve as a major source for knowledge of Ancient Greek mythology, farming techniques, astronomy and social mores.

Howard, Ron

(1954–) US actor, producer and Academy Award-winning Director. Beginning as a child star on television, Ron Howard has spent almost fifty years in the TV and movie business, and is now regarded as one of the world's most 'bankable' movie directors with over twenty movies and numerous TV projects to his credit— including *A Beautiful Mind*, *Apollo 13* and *Cinderella Man*.

Ingersoll, Robert Green

(1833–1899) US political leader, lawyer and orator noted for his broad range of culture and his defense of agnosticism. Rising from virtual poverty to become one of the leading figures of his day, Ingersoll was a powerful orator and a persuasive lawyer who influenced the operation of law in the US in the latter half of the 19th Century and exerted great influence on the country's highest political office, though his strongly-held and controversial views—especially on his agnosticism—meant that he never held public office himself.

Jackson, Jesse Louis

(1941–) US civil rights activist (and follower of Martin Luther King) and Baptist minister. He was a candidate for the Democratic presidential nomination in 1984 and 1988, and is a prominent leader of the American Christian left and spokesman for African-Americans. His son is a US Congressman.

John of Salisbury

(c. 1120–1180) English author, diplomat and bishop of Chartres, born at Salisbury. Being of Saxon descent—not the ruling Normans—it is a tribute to his discipline and intelligence that he rose to prominence in the Church, having moved to France at the age of sixteen. He was influenced by the ancient Greek and Latin thinkers—particularly Plato, whose influences can be seen in his writings. As secretary to Saint Thomas à Becket, he was involved in the conflict between Becket and King Henry II over the rights and position of the Church, and when Becket was murdered by the king's followers, John returned to France. He was made bishop of Chartres in 1176, a post he held until his death.

Jung, Karl Gustav

(1875–1961) Swiss psychiatrist and founder of analytical psychology. Jung's influential approach to psychology stressed understanding the psyche through exploring the worlds of dreams, art, mythology, world religion and philosophy. His most notable contributions include his concept of the psychological archetype, the collective unconscious, and his theory of synchronicity. Jung emphasised the importance of balance and harmony, claiming that rather than relying only on science and logic, we would benefit from integrating spirituality and appreciation of the unconscious realm—in this he was a great influence on the Constructivist movement which has gradually supplanted the Behaviourist approach in psychology.

Kanamaru, Miki

(1972–) Japanese-born, US, Canadian and Australian educated Australian psychologist, counsellor and fine artist. Though respected in the areas of organisational and human resource psychology, her particular gift is in the areas of family and grief-counselling and conflict-resolution strategies.

Kierkegaard, Søren Aabye

(1813–1855) A profound and prolific writer in what has been called the Danish 'golden age' of intellectual and artistic activity. His writings encompassed the domains of philosophy, theology, psychology, literary criticism, devotional literature and fiction. Highly intellectual, he is known as the 'father of existentialism', though his Christian background and his wider writings mark him as falling outside the general description of an existentialist. His influence on later thinkers—even those who did not share his burning Christian faith—cannot be underestimated.

Landy, John Michael, AC, CVO, MBE

(1930–) Australian athlete (world-record holder for the 1500 metres from June 1954–July 1957), naturalist, author and former Governor of the State of Victoria (2001–2006). Landy was the second man in history to run the mile in under 4 minutes (Roger Bannister was the first) and though he never won an Olympic gold medal, he is universally considered one of the great runners of the 1950s.

Lee, Harper

(1926–) US novelist. Known for her Pulitzer Prize-winning 1960 novel *To Kill a Mockingbird*—her only published novel. With *Mockingbird*, Harper Lee achieved fame—and fortune—and wrote what many believe was the greatest American novel of the century and 'a perfectly constructed piece of literature'. Her friendship with Truman Capote—whom she knew as a child, and who is generally accepted to be the model for Dill in the novel—has been depicted in two recent films about the writing of his masterpiece *In Cold Blood*, for which Harper Lee assisted in the research.

Lewin, Roger A.

(1946–) US psychiatrist and author. Dr Lewin born in Cleveland, Ohio, in 1946 and grew up there with some interludes in France. He has had a varied career, including work in Tanzania and Brazil, as well as playing a leading role in the development of an alternative high school in Cleveland. Dr Lewin has written three books on psychiatry: *Losing and Fusing* (with Clarence Schulz, M.D.) *Compassion* and *Creative Collaboration in Psychotherapy*, and two books of poetry, *New Wrinkles* and *Spring Fed Pond*.

Lim, Jeremy

(1990–) Singaporean student and writer. Born with OI (osteogenesis imperfecta)—more commonly known as 'brittle bone disease'—Jeremy has become well known in his native Singapore through his advocacy for disability awareness, his fortnightly newspaper columns, and his numerous personal and television appearances, but mostly for his unflagging confidence and enthusiasm. He has been the Youth Ambassador for the Singapore National Kidney Foundation Children's Medical Fund, and a MindChamps Youth Fellow.

His mother, Wong Liang Ming, is the National Taekwondo Head Coach and a four-time South East Asian Games Champion while his father, Lim Teong Chin, who is also a respected coach, is the only Singaporean to hold an 8th dan blackbelt, recognised by the World Taekwondo Federation.

Luciana, Monica

US Associate Professor of Psychology at the University of Minnesota, specialising in neuropsychology. Dr Luciana studies the brain to discover how emotion, thinking and perception enable or derail working memory and functional behavior.

'Experience can affect people, but it acts on a nervous system that includes neurons and brain chemicals,' she says. 'My major goal is to address how it is that the specific neurochemical systems develop from childhood to adolescence to young adulthood, how they function in healthy people, and how they might be disrupted in clinical disorders.

'Brain chemicals allow most of our behavior to occur, and they are present in all brain regions. The biggest challenge is to understand how integration is achieved across the cognitive (thinking), motivational, and perceptual brain systems that help us function adaptively.'

McCloskey, Robert James

(1922–1996) US Journalist and Diplomat—Ambassador to Cyprus, the Netherlands and Greece. After a short career as a journalist, Robert McCloskey entered the State Department and had a distinguished diplomatic career, which saw him fill three Ambassadorial posts, as well as a period as Assistant Secretary of State for Legislative affairs

Markova, Dawna

US author, psychotherapist, researcher and consultant to leaders of organisations from education to healthcare to corporations. Dawna Markova is an author and a storyteller, with a passion for universal education and change through creativity. Dr Markova has PhDs in psychology and education. She has written seven books including *The Art of the Possible*; *How Your Child Is Smart*; *The Smart Parenting Revolution* and *No Enemies Within*. She is one of the creators of the Random Acts of Kindness Series, and has written for many publications.

Maslow, Abraham

(1908–1970) US psychologist. Famous for his proposal of the 'Hierarchy of Needs' (see Part One, Section 2 and Case Study 1), Maslow was one of the most influential psychologists of the 20th Century.

Newton, Sir Isaac, FRS

(1642–1727) British natural scientist, mathematician and physicist. Acknowledged by many as the 'Father of Modern Physics' and a key figure in the history of mathematics, Newton was responsible for enunciating the laws of motion. He is also credited (along with Gottfried Liebniz) with inventing calculus. In the science of optics, his discoveries include the existence of the white light spectrum and the particle theory of light, and he is perhaps most famous for his theory of gravity upon which most later cosmology and physics is dependant. By any measure, Newton is one of the giants in the history of human thought.

Peter the Hermit

(c. 1050–1115) Also known as Little Peter or Peter of Amiens, Peter the Hermit is considered one of the main instigators of the First Crusade. After Pope Urban II made a speech in 1095, Peter began a tour of France and Germany, preaching the merits of crusade as he went. Raising an army of untrained and disorganised poor people who followed Peter the Hermit most eagerly to Constantinople in what became known as 'The People's Crusade' or 'The Crusade of the Poor People.'

His army was unprepared and badly defeated, and, disheartened, Peter almost returned home. Eventually, however, he made his way to Jerusalem, and just before the city was stormed he preached a sermon on the Mount of Olives. A few years after the capture of Jersualem, Peter the Hermit returned to France, where he established an Augustinian monastery.

Petty, Richard

Distinguished US academic in psychology. Petty's research focuses broadly on the situational and individual difference factors responsible for changes in beliefs, attitudes and behaviors. Much of his current work is aimed at understanding prejudice, consumer choices, political and legal decisions, and health behaviors. Topics of special current interest include: understanding the role of meta-cognitive as well as implicit (unconscious) factors in persuasion and resistance to change; the effect of racial and ethnic prejudice, stereotypes, and specific emotions on social judgment and behavior; and investigating how people correct their evaluations for various factors they think may have biased their judgments (such as stereotypes they hold or emotions they are experiencing). He has written seven books and over 200 articles and book chapters.

Plato

(427–347 BC) Ancient Greek philosopher, teacher and thinker. The central figure in the 'Big Three' (Socrates, Plato and Aristotle) whose ideas have influenced the development of Western thought for almost two-and-a-half thousand years, Plato was a student of Socrates and the founder of the Academy in Athens where Aristotle later studied. Plato wrote on a wide range of philosophical issues in the areas of ethics, politics and history, metaphysics and epistemology. His influential ideas have come down through the survival of his *Dialogues* and letters.

Prescott, James W.

American developmental psychologist, whose research focused on the origins of violence, particularly as it relates to a lack of mother-child bonding. He established a link between neurotic behavior and isolation from a care-giving mother, suggesting that absence of affection in childhood is a major cause of adult violence amongst humans.

In his paper *Body Pleasure and the Origins of Violence*, he presents evidence suggesting that societies open to touch and sexuality suffer from less violence than intolerant societies.

Publilius Syrus

(1st century BC) Assyrian-born Latin writer, who was brought as a slave to Italy, but by his wit and talent won the favor of his master, who freed and educated him. All that remains of his works is a collection of about 700 *Sentences* (*Sententiae*), a series of moral maxims in iambic and trochaic verse. Each maxim is comprised of a single verse, and the verses are arranged in alphabetical order according to their initial letters.

Rogers, Carl

(1902–1987) US psychologist and personality theoretician. Rogers is famous for his work on self-actualisation—the theory that the built-in motivation present in every life form is to develop its potentials to the fullest extent possible, and not simply for survival. Rogers believed that all human beings strive to make the very best of their existence. His theories influenced and are closely tied to those of Abraham Maslow.

Schwartz, Jeffrey M.

(1951–) US M.D., psychiatrist and author. An internationally recognised authority on Obsessive Compulsive Disorder (OCD)—see his book *Brain Lock*—Schwartz is a proponent of the concept that the conscious will has the power to physically alter the structure of the brain. This concept is explored in detail in his book (co-written with Sharon Begley) *The Mind & the Brain: Neuroplasticity and the Power of Mental Force* (New York: ReganBooks, Harper Collins, 2002).

Schweitzer, Albert, MD, OM.

(1875–1965) Alsatian (from Alsace-Lorraine), later French, Nobel Peace Prize-winning doctor, humanitarian, theologian, philosopher and musician. His work in theology influenced the mid-20th Century view of Christ's role, and he was a famous organist with a fascination for the works of Bach, but his greatest fame—and his Nobel Prize—was for his humanitarian work in Africa, particularly his building and running of the Lambaréné hospital in Gabon on the central west coast of the continent.

Seligman, Martin E.P.
US psychologist and author. Martin Seligman is a globally-recognised authority on 'learned helplessness' and 'learned optimism'. He is also the 'face and the founding father' of the positive psychology movement. His books, Authentic Happiness, Learned Helplessness, Learned Optimism, What You Can Change and What You Can't and The Optimistic Child are invaluable contributions to our understanding of the constructive effect of positive psychological principles in our treatment of children—and adults.

Seneca, Lucius Annaeus
(3BC–65 AD) Ancient Roman orator, writer and dramatist. Born in Spain, he was a brilliant youth, studying law and the Greek poets. Exiled by Caligula, he wrote eight tragedies, which remain the only surviving specimens of Latin tragic drama. On the death of Caligula, he returned to Rome and became the tutor of the young Nero. In the early years of Nero's rule, Seneca was himself very powerful in Rome.

Shakespeare, William
(1564–1616) English playwright and poet. Arguably the greatest literary figure in the history of Western literature, Shakespeare is the most-quoted writer of all time. He wrote 38 plays, excelling at comedy, tragedy and historical themes, and composed 159 poems—154 of them sonnets on a variety of themes. His influence on later English literature and his 'coinages' give Shakespeare an indelible place in the history of letters.

Shaw, George Bernard
(1856–1950) World-renowned Irish author and dramatist. Shaw was self-educated, rejecting traditional education, for which he had a lifelong contempt. His most notable success was in drama. His work is liberally laced with humour, but with a strong spine of social commentary and strong messages to which audiences can relate.

A dedicated socialist, he wrote many brochures and speeches for the Fabian Society advocating equal rights for men and women and for the under-classes. He remains one of only two people to have been awarded both a Nobel Prize (1925) (for his contribution to Literature) and an Academy Award (1938) for *Pygmalion*.

Shyamalan, M. Night (Manoj Nelliattu)

(1970–) Indian-born US Academy Award nominated film director, screenwriter and actor. With a string of popular movies since 1999—including *The Sixth Sense, Unbreakable, The Village* and *Lady in the Water,* Shyamalan explores the supernatural and spiritual elements of human imagination within very ordinary settings, and is noted for his 'twist' endings. He also performs smaller roles in his own movies.

Snyder, Allan Whitenack, FRS

US-born Australian research scientist and lecturer. A Fellow of the Royal Society, the multi-award-winning director of the Centre for the Mind holds the Peter Karmel Chair of Science and the Mind at The Australian National University, where he is also Head of the Optical Science Centre and Professor of Visual Science and Optical Physics. At the University of Sydney, he holds the 150th Anniversary Chair of Science and the Mind. Allan Snyder's work in vision and optics—which has been described as 'breaking the 19th Century mindset'—is behind three main branches of science. These are optical fibre telecommunications, visual photoreceptor optics and futuristic light-guiding-light technologies. His 'brave and original' work on the potential of the human brain has been described in the *New York Times* as 'a breakthrough that could lead to a revolution in the way we understand... the functioning of the human brain'.

Socrates

(470–399 BC) Ancient Greek philosopher, scientist and teacher. Known as 'the Father of Western Philosophy', none of Socrates actual writings have survived, and we know of his thoughts only through the writings of his contemporaries and his students. In fact, there is some question as to Socrates' actual existence—some commentators and historians regarding him more as an idea or an 'authority of reference' than as an actual historical personage. Whether this suggestion can ever be proved or disproved is an open question, but there can be no doubt that the teachings ascribed to Socrates by Plato, Aristophanes and other famous Athenians were the basis of philosophy, methods of scientific enquiry, ethics and aesthetics in Europe and throughout the world for well over two thousand years.

Stapp, Henry

US quantum physicist, working out of the University of California's Lawrence Berkeley National Laboratory. One aspect of Stapp's work looks at the implications of quantum mechanics for consciousness. Though complex and unintelligible to most lay-people, one of the key aspects of Stapp's theory is that, in quantum terms (acknowledging what has become known as Quantum Darwinism) each increase in individual (and, hence, cumulative) human knowledge is associated with an 'act of creation' (resulting from a 'wave function collapse'), which represents a step along the arrow of time. Thus, free will could be seen as resulting from, and directly instrumental in, the evolution of the universe.

Terence (Publius Terentius Afer)

(circa 190–158 BC) Ancient Roman playwright. Probably a native of Carthage, Terence was a slave in the family of a Roman patrician (aristocrat). Because of his witty conversation and graceful manners, he became a favourite in the fashionable society of Rome and was granted his freedom. He became one of the most important dramatists of his time, writing polished and sophisticated comedies, mainly for the aristocracy.

Twain, Mark (Samuel Langhorne Clemens)

(1835–1910) US author, satirist and lecturer. An extremely popular writer both during his lifetime and since, Mark Twain was a master of colloquial speech and had the unique ability to combine strong storytelling with humour and social criticism in a way which made him one of the most influential of all American writers. He had a passionate interest in science, and formed a firm friendship with inventor Nikola Tesla—one of the 19th and early 20th Century's most innovative and creative scientific minds. Mark Twain's most famous books are *The Adventures of Huckleberry Finn*, *The Adventures of Tom Sawyer*, *A Connecticut Yankee in King Arthur's Court* and *The Prince and the Pauper*.

Van Buren, Abigail (real name, Pauline Esther Friedman Phillips)

(1918–) Abigail Van Buren is the pseudonym (or pen-name) used by Pauline Esther Friedman Phillips, the original writer of the widely syndicated *Dear Abby* column. When she began writing the column during 1956, she used the pseudonym of Abigail Van Buren and she has used the name ever since. Phillips arrived at the name by combining the name of the biblical character Abigail, mentioned in the Book of Samuel, with the last name of former US President Martin Van Buren. Her successor in the role of Dear Abby since 2002 has been her daughter Jeanne Phillips—who uses the same pen-name.

Whitman, Walt (Walter)

(1819–1892) US poet, journalist, essayist and humanist philosopher. Translated into over 25 languages, Whitman's poetry is among the most influential and best loved in the American canon. His style was seen as controversial (even iconoclastic) during his lifetime, but has, in the succeeding century, influenced the style of later poets and writers, both in the US and overseas.

Wilde, Oscar Fingal O'Flahertie Wills

(1854–1900) Irish playwright, novelist and poet and short story author. Known for his incisive wit, he was one of the most successful playwrights of late Victorian London, and one of the greatest celebrities of his day. A homosexual, he suffered a dramatic downfall as the result of a famous trial, and was imprisoned for two years of hard labour after being convicted of the offence of gross indecency.

Woods, (Eldrick) Tiger

(1975–) US professional golfer. Tiger Woods was a child prodigy, who began playing golf at the age of two. Already ranked as one of the greatest golfers of all time, Woods, due to his relative youth and dominance of his sport, is predicted to break all records for tournament wins and prize money. His record of awards and 'all-time' achievements is already too long to list here. Woods' multi-racial (African-American and Asian) heritage has led to a surge in popularity of the game, which was once thought of as remote and elitist.

How to Use This Series:

The Art of Communicating with Your Child is the second volume in the *MindChamps®' Better Parenting Collection™*, a collection designed to provide parents and teachers with a comprehensive approach to preparing children, academically, socially, emotionally and creatively, for life as citizens in the world-community of the 21st Century.

Volume I

'Deeper than the Ocean': The Ingredients of the 'Champion Mindset'

Provides the scientific, psychological and philosophical underpinnings for the creation of a forward-focused and creative 'Champion Mindset'—the mindset which will prepare the young person for success in the world of the 21st Century. This is the essential knowledge-base, upon which the following volumes will build, to create the supportive and productive home environment—the 'Home Nation'—or a more effective approach to constructing learning strategies within the classroom setting.

Volume II

'The Art of Communicating with Your Child': How to Inspire the 'Champion Mindset' in Children

Builds upon the understandings of Volume I to develop the practical skills and techniques, encompassing a number of key areas for ensuring optimal communication with your child. These key areas include: interpersonal communications, developing self-concept and self-respect, moral and ethical maturity. Superior communication between parent and child is one of the key factors for developing a successful citizen of the future—a future-focused individual with the mindset of a champion.

Volume III

'The Art of Learning How to Learn': How to Prepare Your Child's Mind for the 21st Century

Focuses on the 'New Brain Software™'—a comprehensive suite of Ideation Techniques and Advanced Whole-Brain Learning Strategies (Active Understanding; Information Control Strategies and Research Skills for the 'Information-Saturated' Modern World and Active Recall Strategies for the effective storage of new understandings). In addition, it describes in detail the Optimal Flow Method™ of learning, which ties all these concepts together.

Volume IV
'The Art of Creative Thinking': How to Unlock your Child's Amazing Creativity.

Looks in detail at human creativity. Creativity has the reputation for being 'mysterious' and out of reach to the 'average person', but, in fact, we all possess the power and the 'hardware' for creativity if we learn how to access it. Volume IV demystifies the creative process, making its 'secrets' easily accessible to parents and teachers. It draws on Creativity Theory, the strategies of the greatest creative minds throughout history and the ground-breaking research of The Centre for the Mind to create a comprehensive approach to developing, in all children, the creativity which will become the key to building a successful future in the 'Century of the Mind'.

The MindChamps®' Better Parenting Collection is an ambitious project, and it is one which has been many years in the making. It takes the reader on a unique journey through the disparate, yet significantly interrelated, realms of neuroscience, cognitive psychology and learned optimism, metaphor and story, self-esteem building and creativity strategies, and practical educational and communication techniques—providing background and strategies for the parent's/teacher's role as guide and facilitator of our children's future.

Now, more than ever before, young people need strong and informed leadership from trusted adults to get closer to 'the truth' among the many versions of 'reality' which surround them in today's media-dominated society.

Volume I, *Deeper than the Ocean*, introduces many of the key concepts. Volumes II, III and IV are designed to take the mystery out of the growth and learning process and lift the lid on the 'secret strategies' of creative thinkers.

It is recommended that on your first reading, you work your way through each volume in order. The insights and the practical applications build upon what has gone before, and arguments or suggestions will make far more sense if you are familiar with the previously-introduced concepts and research.

Working through each chapter step-by-step gives you a detailed overview of the landscape of the young person's mind, and the best way to fulfil our responsibilities as guides on their journey towards the future.

It is not an easy task to understand the breadth of this wide-ranging topic, but drawing on experience and research in a variety of areas, this collection is designed to do what few (if any) have done before. It is designed to make the intricacies and the needs of the learning brain accessible to a wide range of readers—parents, teachers and anyone who is interested in making a difference to the lives of the young.

Companion Volumes

As well as the four main volumes, we will be releasing, from time to time, companion volumes—books which develop particular aspects of the themes introduced in the main collection and include practical advice and activities for parents with children of different ages or development levels. The first two of these will be *The 3-Mind Revolution* and *Building the Home Nation*.